Geographic Information System

Modeling and Measuring Techniques

Geographic Information System

Modeling and Measuring Techniques

Akash Deep Sharma

MD Publications Pvt Ltd
New Delhi
www.mdppl.com

Published by
MD Publications Pvt Ltd
"MD House", 11, Darya Ganj,
New Delhi-110002
Ph. : +91-11-41563325, 41562846
E-mail : **contact@mdppl.com**
Website : **www.mdppl.com**

ISBN : 978-81-7533-115-0

PRICE : Rs. 695.00

Published and Printed by
MD Publications Pvt Ltd at Printext,
D2/149A, Jeewan Park, Uttam Nagar, New Delh.

PREFACE

A Geographic Information System is a set of information transformation tools that derive new geographic datasets from existing datasets. These geoprocessing functions take information from existing datasets, apply analytic functions, and write results into new derived datasets. Geographic Information System is a computer system for capturing, storing, checking, integrating, manipulating, analysing and displaying data related to positions on the earth's surface. Typically a Geographic Information System also known as Spatial Information Systems is used for handling maps of one kind or another. These might be represented as several different layers where each layer holds data about a particular kind of feature. Each feature is linked to a position on the graphical image of a map. Layers of data are organised to be studied and to perform statistical analysis. A GIS is a computer system capable of capturing, storing, analyzing, and displaying geographically referenced information; that is, data identified according to location. Practitioners also define a GIS as including the procedures, operating personnel, and spatial data that go into the system.

The power of a GIS comes from the ability to relate different information in a spatial context and to reach a conclusion about this relationship. Most of the information we have about our world contains a location reference, placing that information at some point on the globe. When rainfall information is collected, it is important to know where the rainfall is located. This is done by using a location reference system, such as longitude and latitude, and perhaps elevation. Comparing the rainfall information with other information, such as the location of marshes across the landscape, may show that certain marshes receive little rainfall. This fact may indicate that these marshes are likely to dry up, and this inference can help us make the most appropriate decisions about how humans should interact with the marsh. A GIS, therefore, can reveal important new information that leads to better decision making.

Many computer databases that can be directly entered into a GIS are being produced by Federal, State, tribal, and local governments, private companies, academia, and nonprofit organizations. Different kinds of data in map form can be entered into a GIS. A GIS can also convert existing digital information, which may not yet be in map form, into forms it can recognize and use. For example, digital satellite images can be analyzed to produce a map of digital information about land use and land cover. Likewise, census or hydrologic tabular data can be converted to a map like form and serve as layers of thematic information in a GIS.

A GIS can be used to emphasize the spatial relationships among the objects being mapped. While a computer-aided mapping system may represent a road simply as a line, a GIS may also recognize that road as the boundary between wetland and urban development between two census statistical areas. Data capture putting the information into the system involves identifying the objects on the map, their absolute location on the Earth's surface, and their spatial relationships. Software tools that automatically extract features from satellite images or aerial photographs are gradually replacing what has traditionally been a time-consuming capture process. Objects are identified in a series of attribute tables the "information" part of a GIS.

A property ownership map might be at a different scale than a soils map. Map information in a GIS must be manipulated so that it registers, or fits, with information gathered from other maps.

Projection is a fundamental component of mapmaking. A projection is a mathematical means of transferring information from the Earth's three-dimensional, curved surface to a two-dimensional medium paper or a computer screen. Different projections are used for different types of maps because each projection is particularly appropriate for certain uses. For example, a projection that accurately represents the shapes of the continents will distort their relative sizes. The use of a GIS can encourage cooperation and communication among the organizations involved in environmental protection, planning, and resource management. The collection of data for a GIS is costly. Data collection can require very specialized computer equipment and technical expertise.

Thanks to Mr. Pranav Gupta of **MD Publications Pvt Ltd,** New Delhi, who supported me fully for completing this book.

Akash Deep Sharma

Contents

1

Geographic Information System: Definition and Meaning

Introduction

The use of Geographic Information Systems (GIS) was limited to a small number of research and applications users. Today, GIS is one of the fastest growing technologies; it has applications in public safety, natural resource management, environmental analysis, utilities, and government, and is moving quickly into many other areas. The motivation for the tremendous growth in the use of GIS is clearly linked to both the increasing demand for information and the ever-increasing ability of computer technology to provide effective, cost-efficient data processing and management capabilities.

Conceptually, a GIS can be envisioned as a stacked set of map layers, where each layer is aligned or registered to all other layers. Typically, each layer will contain a unique geographic theme or data type. These themes might include, for example, topography, soils, land-use, cadastral (land ownership) information, or infrastructure such as roads, pipelines, power lines, or sewer networks. This image of GIS is shown in Figure 1. By sharing mutual geography, all layers in the GIS can be combined or overlaid in any user-specified combination. In some cases the GIS may be defined by the type of data that the system is designed to handle. For example, the term "Land Information System" or "LIS" is often applied to a type of GIS used by counties, cities, and municipalities to manage land parcel information.

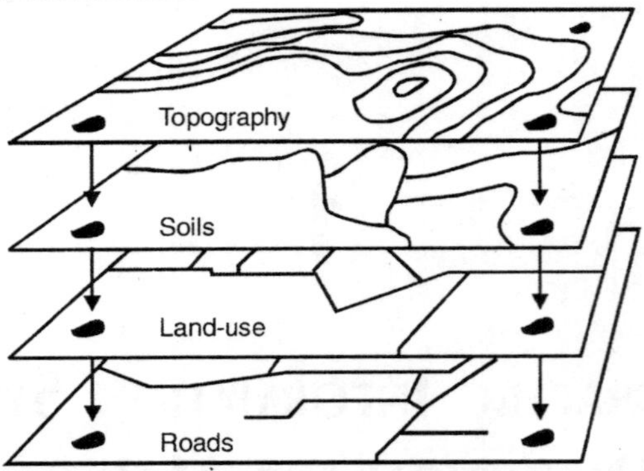

Figure 1.1. A conceptual model of a GIS provides a useful way to visualize GIS as a set of map layers or themes, all registered together to a common map base or geographic area. Each layer typically contains one type of data. The GIS database stores both the spatial data (where something occurs) and the attribute data (characteristics of the data) for all of the features shown on each layer.

In some of its simpler operations, GIS provides an automated version of traditional map analysis. Map overlay is probably the most common GIS function; this function has long been performed manually or optically using maps registered over light tables or via photographic techniques. In GIS, however, the number of registered map layers that can be collected and stored is theoretically infinite. The user can quickly retrieve, overlay, manipulate, and analyze any number or combination of layers. The user can then assess the results of the analysis on a computer screen or on a hard copy paper map produced by the GIS, or can summarize the results in a tabular format. However simple or complex the user's purpose, a GIS is used to access an integrated, geographically referenced database of maps that can be overlaid, combined, and analyzed to user specifications.

Because GIS is a rapidly growing technology, many different definitions of GIS now exist. A very useful definition of GIS that we will adopt in this publication is a true systems-based definition: *a GIS is a computerized, integrated system used to compile, store, manipulate, and output mapped spatial data.* Later in this publication, this definition will be discussed in detail. The intended audience for this publication includes GIS novices as well as those who are interested in getting started with GIS. By exploring this systems-based definition and expanding on it, you will be given a succinct, yet comprehensive view of this technology.

Our systems-based definition may be called "functional" because it is based on the functions that a GIS performs. Since each of these functions is performed on the geographic data associated with the GIS, the definition may also be called "data-centered."

Another way to understand GIS is to examine the generic "components" that the system must contain. Thus, in addition to data, a true GIS includes computer hardware, software, and users. In order to accurately be called a GIS, a system must contain all of these elements. This is a crucial distinction. Note that the acquisition of a software package or a set of computer hardware does not mean that the user has a "GIS." Similarly, merely computerizing a set of mapped data does not result in a "GIS." An actual GIS includes all of the essential elements of data, technology, and people who use the system in support of data management and analysis. You should be aware that there are several technologies that are related to GIS but are not the same as GIS. Table 1 names and defines several of these technologies.

Advances in computer technology to support data management and analysis have simultaneously occurred in areas other than mapped or spatial data processing and so a number of technologies that are somewhat similar to GIS have become established. These technologies include Computer Assisted Drawing and Drafting (CADD) systems, Database Management Systems (DBMS), and Automated Mapping/Facilities Management (AM/FM) systems. Each of these technologies has been developed for specific purposes, such as the use of CADD systems for the generation of architectural drawings for a new building. Yet a clear distinction can be drawn between GIS and these other technologies because GIS has evolved exclusively to manage and analyze mapped data. The ability of GIS to predicate all data processing functions on geographic location makes this technology distinct. These data processing functions include not only the storage and communication of mapped data, but also the measurement and analysis of data portrayed on maps.

Table 1.1. Several technologies are related to GIS but are not the same as GIS.

NAME	ACRONYM	USES
Computer Assisted Drawing and Drafting	CADD	Drawing packages used to generate and produce digitally compiled drawings. CADD data are often not geographic (mapped). Some data developed in CADD systems can be incorporated into a GIS.
Automated Mapping/ Facilities Management	AM/FM	Computerized map generation software that is most often utilized for infrastructure analysis and management. Similar to LIS technology.
Database Management System	DBMS	Software packages used to manage and analysis attribute data. Not used specifically for map analysis. Some GIS packages use DBMS to handle data management tasks.
Computer/Automated Cartography	C/AC	Computer software used automatically generate maps. Does not include integrated database or data analysis capabilities of GIS
Image Processing	IP	Sets of computerized routines used for information extraction (e.g., pattern recognition and classification) from remotely sensed images. Output from IP systems is often used as input to a GIS
Land Information System	LIS	Type of GIS that manages and analyzes data related to land ownership (e.g., tax parcels, urban infrastructure, property assessment).
Spatial Decision Support System	SDSS	A customized computer-based information system that utilizes decision rules and models and incorporates spatial data. These systems are often built from GIS databases, and may employ a subset of GIS funtionality to meet user requirments.

Both the components required for GIS and the functional definition of GIS provide a useful way to approach this technology. After systematically examining each component and function, you can then conceptually re-integrate the individual parts into a complete whole. This approach, termed decomposition, will give you a full understanding of the system.

Before examining the individual components and functions of GIS, it will be helpful to consider the nature of maps and mapped data. A GIS works with observations or measurements that can be tied to a specific geographic location on the ground. Another common term for mapped data is spatial data. Spatial data vary with location, so the nature of the data that we collect, measure, and interpret will change as we consider various locations on the earth's surface. Observations of the earth's surface are recorded on maps to portray the spatial data in a format that is easy for humans to comprehend. Maps, as devices used to communicate the nature of spatial data, are the focus of the next section.

Maps and Map Data Handling

Maps are fundamental tools used to portray spatial or geographic data. Data shown on maps vary with location. Map data are organized, classified, and depicted in a manner chosen by the map maker to optimize the map's effectiveness in communicating the nature of the data. When we read a map, we are looking for patterns, linkages, or relationships in the map's data. In some cases, we may look at several maps simultaneously to determine relationships between geographic data depicted on those separate maps.

All maps are simplifications of the real world. The true earth is infinitely complex and it is not possible to depict on a map all of the real earth features that we might be interested in. As a simplified image of the earth, maps can be called models of reality. Though they are simplifications, these models are quite sophisticated, and the science of map making, called cartography, is a formal geographic science.

Cartographers design and produce maps using very rigid rules and guidelines. A true map must accurately show not only what the nature of the mapped variable is (in correct proportion), but also must correctly place all mapped data in their true geographic locations. The geographic location of spatial data can be classified into two types: absolute and relative. Absolute location refers to a unique and standardized place or position, while relative location defines position based on the location of other variables or phenomena. Absolute geographic position is specified using a universal coordinate system such as Latitude/Longitude or Universal Transverse Mercator(UTM) coordinates. These universal coordinate systems allow both the map maker and the map user to specify a unique and definite position for every location on both the earth and maps of the earth. This unique location, which is "tagged" to all spatial data, is critical to being able to store and analyze data in a GIS. It is this geographic tag or characteristic that distinguishes GIS as a technology that focuses on mapped data.

When we read a map, we rarely depend on absolute geographic information to assess patterns or relationships. In consulting a road map, for example, to decide on a route between Los Angeles and San Francisco, the traveler would probably not need to know the coordinates (e.g., latitude/longitude) of each city to select a travel route. Rather, the traveler would visualize the optional routes and come to some decision based on a personal interpretation of the "best" route. In selecting a route by looking at the geographical network of roads connecting the two cities, a casual map user would not seek a formal interpretation of the map. However, even a casual user would assume that all roads and other data depicted on the map are shown in their correct relative positions. Also, this type of user would assume that all mileage and other ancillary data such as the locations of rest stops were accurately reported on the map legend.

For a map to be geographically correct and correctly portray relationships between, for example, roads and cities, the cartographer must follow precise guidelines when compiling the map. For our purposes, we will simplify that set of rules to three parameters: coordinate systems, projections, and scale. Only when these three parameters are specified can a correct map be generated. In turn, an accurate GIS database depends on the availability and use of correct original map manuscripts.

These mapping guidelines prove essential when we convert traditional maps into computerized, GIS-compatible data sets. By specifying locations according to coordinate systems, a robust and accurate GIS can be established. Without a common set of geographic coordinates, layers in a GIS will not register (i.e., overlay precisely), thus precluding any type of multiple map operation such as overlaying two or more maps.

In turn, the ability to generate good location data is based on the accurate projection of the original map data. Projection is the process of transforming locations on the curved earth surface to locations on a two-dimensional plane. This mathematical step is performed by the cartographer to ensure geographic fidelity. While most of us never consider such a seemingly irrelevant source of error as the curvature of the earth, it is a critical consideration to the cartographer, and ultimately but perhaps unknowingly, to the conscientious map user.

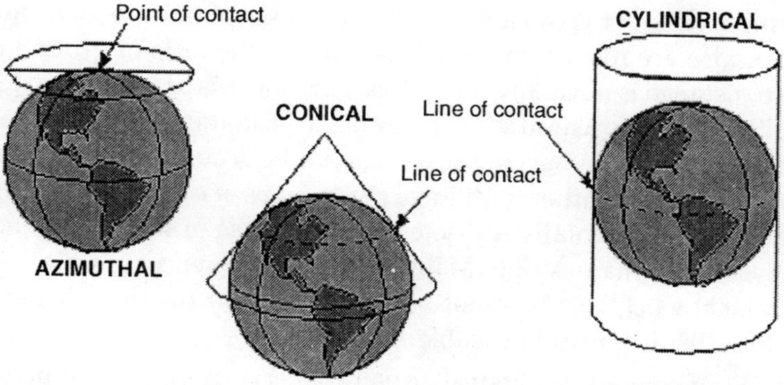

Figure 1.2. Generally there are three classes or families of map projections. Each geometric shape is used to transform the globe (a curved surface) to a plane (the map surface). These three families are called "developable" surfaces because planes, cones, and cylinders can be "flattened" without distortion. Azimuthal or planar projections use a flat two-dimensional surface to develop the map, conical projections are transformed onto a cone wrapped around the globe which is then flattened, and the cylindrical family of maps are projected onto a cylinder wrapped around the globe. Different projections are selected to minimize specific types of distortions in distance, direction, shape and area found on all flat maps.

Few GIS users will actually perform map projection or create a map from scratch. It is more likely that users will compile data from an existing map base, suchas that provided by the U.S. Geological

Survey's (USGS) National Mapping Program. Fortunately, these standard map series conform to rigid accuracy standards. Furthermore, the margin of each map contains information regarding the projection and coordinate systems that were used. Thus, USGS maps often provide a basis for the generation of other GIS data layers. As GIS developers build their system, and as users access and manipulate data from multiple maps, each must be aware of the need to standardize these parameters. Common projection and coordinate systems for all spatial data must be established if the map data in any GIS are to be fully integrated and registered.

GIS developers and users must also concern themselves with map scale. Scale is the mathematical relationship of real earth distance (ground distance) to that same distance as it is shown on a map. This relationship is often stated as a ratio of the two distances. As mentioned above, all maps are models or simplifications of reality. Maps also are reductions of reality. That is, the ratio of ground to map distance is normally much less than one. Maps to be stored in a GIS must be similar in scale if they are to be manipulated together. Maps with widely varying scales cannot be accurately combined. Thus, the user of either traditional paper maps or computerized GIS maps is fundamentally restricted by the degree of scale difference between map manuscripts. Maps with large differences in scale (e.g., 1:250,000 vs. 1:9,600) cannot be registered and overlaid without serious distortion and probable error.

A GIS converts traditional (usually paper) maps into a computer-compatible form. In order that the spatial data stored in the GIS be accurate, the map maker and the GIS user must consider issues of coordinate systems, projections, and scale. Every GIS requires that data be compatible with respect to these basic issues used in compiling mapped data.

As suggested by the example of the traveler selecting a route between two cities, often our analysis of the data shown on maps is informal. In other cases map users want specific measurements of the relationships between map features. Traditional map analysis is based on manual methods such as the use of a dot grid to measure area or a planimeter to measure distance or area. One of the most significant advantages afforded by a GIS is the ability to automate map analysis functions. That is, a GIS can be used to quantitatively assess the nature of spatial data stored in a GIS map database. These types of GIS operations are discussed in a companion publication, *Introduction to Data Analysis Using Geographic Information Systems.*

Traditional maps suffer some disadvantages over the maps that have been entered (automated) into a GIS, as outlined in Table 1.2. Traditional maps are static and fixed with respect not only to the data, but also with respect to projection, scale, and coordinate system. When a user needs to integrate maps of different scales, for example, it is often necessary to re-draft the maps. Map updates may similarly require a tedious manual process. Users also face practical limits on the number of maps that can be manually overlaid, using a light table for example. Similarly, it is difficult to combine multiple map sheets together into a seamless mosaic of maps which covers an area of interest that extends to more than one map sheet or manuscript. In short, a GIS is able to overcome some of the disadvantages of traditional map management and analysis.

Table 1.2. Advantages and disadvantages of traditional maps compared with GIS.

TRADITIONAL MAPS	GEOGRAPHIC INFORMATION SYSTEMS
Data are static	Data easy to update
Fixed projection, scale, coordinate system	Can convert to new, scale, scale or coordinate system
Quantitative analyses often tedious	Many manipulation options for analyzing maps
Difficult to combine multiple map sheets	Easy to combine multiple map layers
Overlays are restricted to a few layers	Can overlay as many maps as contained in database
Updates require re-drafting	Tools allow for map updates without re-drafting
Difficult to copy and share between many users	Multiple, simultaneous user access available
Lower overhead costs	Higher overhead costs
Paper maps usable in present form	Must convert map data to a digital environment
Few Changes in technology	Technology changes rapidly

We have established the fact that GIS is a multi-faceted, computerized set of techniques for dealing with spatial data. The conceptual model of a GIS as a set of registered map layers is a useful way to visualize GIS. Furthermore, you can now appreciate that the accuracy of the data on any one map as well as the ability to overlay or combine multiple maps is based on cartographic parameters such as scale and coordinate system. The next two sections discuss in depth the components and functions of GIS. This decomposition of GIS into its component parts and functions will give you a basic understanding of what constitutes a GIS as well as what a GIS is used for.

Components of GIS

A common misconception is that data alone constitute a GIS. Similarly, it is sometimes assumed that someone who has purchased GIS software has acquired a "GIS." A central tenet of this publication is that a GIS is a system; it consists of more than just data and software. As a system, it exists to answer geographical or spatial questions, and the answers that it provides support decision-making. Thus, it is not enough to have data, or hardware, or software, or users; all components must be present in the system to have a true, fully-functional GIS.

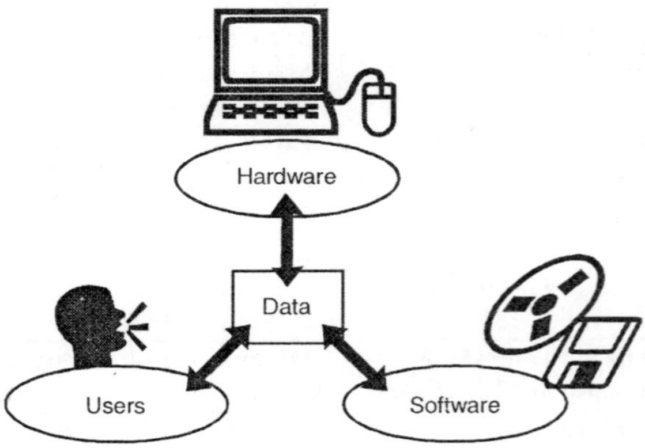

Figure 1.3. Components of a GIS include more than just computer technology. A GIS is an integrated system of users, data, hardware, and software. Data tend to be at the center of any GIS system, while the computer components of the system support data management and analysis.

There are four components of GIS: (1) **data**, (2) **hardware**, (3) **software**, and (4) **users**. The components must be integrated; they must be linked together and work in concert to support the management and analysis of spatial or mapped data.

Data

GIS components are dynamic; there is rapid change in the computer industry as well as turnover of personnel involved in GIS projects. For this reason, GIS developers are often encouraged to adopt a data-centered approach. Simply stated, a data-centered approach views data as the central resource in the GIS. Though data may be shared among multiple users and multiple hardware/ software environments, the data are collected and compiled by a person or organization to support the goal of that user. The other components provide the support needed to process that data.

All data in a GIS are either **spatial** data or **attribute** data. As discussed above, spatial data tells us **where** something occurs. Attribute data tells **what** occurs; it tells us the nature or characteristics of the spatial data. For example, we might describe the location of a municipal water well as a point with the coordinates "45 degrees 17 minutes 20 seconds north latitude, 94 degrees 7 minutes 48 seconds west longitude." Furthermore, we can observe and report several attributes of that well, including its depth, yield, water quality, and proximity to a pumping station. Every GIS provides the ability to store and manipulate both the spatial data and the associated attribute data.

Hardware

Computer hardware used to support GIS is a highly variable part of the overall system. Users will customize their hardware environment to best meet their own individual needs. In all cases, however, a fully-functional GIS must contain hardware to support data input, output, storage, retrieval, display, and analysis. During its infancy, GIS processing was supported only on large mainframe computers. Today, a variety of platforms support GIS processing, ranging from large mainframe computers to mini-computers to scientific work stations to personal computers. In many cases, hardware used to support other applications (e.g., payroll or accounting or digital image processing) is also used for GIS. Hardware configurations for GIS span a tremendous range in terms of start-up and acquisition costs. All systems carry associated costs for maintenance and support.

Software

Software is also a highly dynamic part of the system. Dozens of GIS software packages now exist. These systems are available on many different types of hardware platforms and come with a wide variety of functional capabilities. Public domain software is also available, though on a more limited basis than commercial software. The range in software options goes from generic turn-key systems that are ready for use "right out of the box" to customized installations designed to support specific user needs.

Given the sometimes bewildering array of choices for hardware and software, selection and use of a GIS should be approached strategically. In all cases, anyone considering a GIS software package should consider needs carefully and consult various references, including other users, vendors, and technical publications.

Users

The final component required for a true GIS is users. The term "user" may refer to any individual who will use GIS to support project or program goals, or to an entire organization that will employ GIS in support of its overall mission.

GIS users are often envisioned as hands-on computer processing people. While this is in part true, we choose to define a broader spectrum of GIS users. One classification scheme classifies users into two groups: **system users** and **end users**.

System users are those persons who have actual hands-on use of the GIS hardware and software. These persons have advanced technical skills in the application of GIS to problem solving. System users tend to be responsible not only for the day-to-day use of the system, but also for system maintenance and upkeep.

End users are those persons who do not have actual hands-on use of the system but who do make use of the information products generated via the GIS. End users do not necessarily have to possess hands-on technical skills. However, they must be able to communicate effectively and interact with system users in order to make requests for information products, and must also understand the limitations and requirements of GIS-based processing. GIS must not be a "black box" to end users. They should always be aware of the costs and benefits of a GIS approach to problem solving in order to determine if the requests they make of GIS are reasonable and to judge the quality of the output they receive.

Yet another type of user can be called **data generators**. These are people who collect the raw data to be entered into the GIS. Because a GIS requires such a strict structuring of the data (refer to Maps and Map Data Handling), data generators must often predicate data collection and compilation on the demands of the GIS. Thus, these persons must be made aware that the intended use of the GIS will play a major role in the way that they collect and package data.

In sum, we can see that there is a broad spectrum of GIS users, a spectrum that extends beyond the image of all users as "hands-on" GIS experts. GIS has the capacity to affect people at all stages of the data collection, management, manipulation, and interpretation process.

Functions of GIS

Another productive way to study GIS is through our original definition: a GIS is a computerized, integrated system used to compile, store, manipulate, and output mapped data. This section examines each of these functions.

Compilation

Data compilation involves assembling all of the spatial and attribute data that are to be stored in a computerized format within the GIS. Map data with common projections, scales, and coordinate systems must be pulled together in order to establish the centralized GIS database. Data must also be examined for compatibility in terms of content and time of data collection. Ultimately, the data will be stored in a GIS according to the specific format requirements set by both the user and the chosen GIS software/hardware environment.

When all of the common data requirements are set by the GIS user, a "base map" has been established. A base map is a set of standard requirements for data. It provides accurate standards for geographic control, and also defines a model or template that is used to shape all data into a compatible form. A base map is not necessarily a map per se; rather, it is a comprehensive set of standards established and enacted to ensure quality control for the spatial and attribute data contained in the GIS.

Once the data are assembled and base map parameters are set, the user must translate the map and attribute data into computer-compatible form. This conversion process, referred to as "conversion" or "digitizing," converts paper maps into numerical digits that can be stored in the computer. Digitizing can be performed using various techniques. Scanning is one technique. Another technique is line digitizing which uses a tablet and a tracing stylus. Digitizing simplifies map data into sets of points, lines, or cells that can be stored in the GIS computer. Each GIS software package will impose a specific form and design on the way that these sets of points, lines, and cells are stored as digital map files.

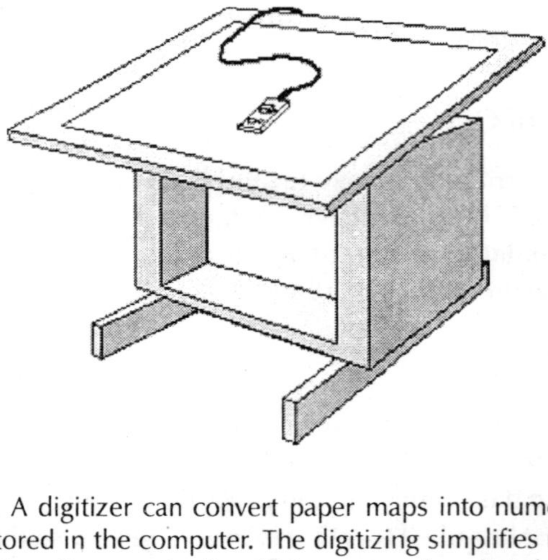

Figure 1.4. A digitizer can convert paper maps into numerical digits that can be stored in the computer. The digitizing simplifies map data into sets of points, lines, and cells which are stored as digital map files.

Digitization is a simplification process that converts all spatial data to either a point (e.g., a well), a line (e.g., a stream), a polygon formed by a closed, complex line (e.g., a lake), or a grid cell. Digitization reduces all spatial entities to these simple forms because they are easy to store in the computer. A GIS database cannot readily recognize features or entities as human map users do. For example, we cannot enter the entity "lake" into a GIS. Rather, we enter the spatial data coordinates for the lake's shoreline as a polygon. Later, the attributes of the lake will be entered into the GIS database and will be associated with the polygon.

Following the digitization of map features, the user completes the compilation phase by relating all spatial features to their respective attributes, and by cleaning up and correcting errors introduced as a result of the data conversion process. The end result of compilation is a set of digital files, each accurately representing all of the spatial and attribute data of interest contained on the original map manuscripts. These digital files contain geographic coordinates for spatial objects (points, lines, polygons, and cells) that represent mapped features. Although we conceptualize the GIS as a set of registered map layers, the GIS actually stores these data at a much more primitive level.

Storage

Once the data have been digitally compiled, digital map files in the GIS are stored on magnetic or other (e.g., optical) digital media. Again, different GIS software packages will employ different storage formats. In most cases, however, data storage will be based on a generic data model that is used to convert map data into a digital form. The two most common types of data models are **raster** and **vector**. Both types are used to simplify the data shown on a map into a more basic form that can be easily and efficiently stored in the computer.

Raster

Raster approaches to storing map data in a GIS are perhaps the most intuitive. Figure 1.5 shows the essential steps involved in converting a map to a raster format. First, a gridded matrix is registered to and overlaid on the original map manuscript. Location in the grid is defined by the row and column coordinates of each cell. To encode the map data for each cell in the raster format, three pieces of data are recorded: the **row coordinate**, the **column coordinate**, and the **attribute**. Thus a triplet of data is recorded for each cell in the array, which is termed a raster. After map data are stored in a raster format, each cell in the raster corresponds to a location on the map and each cell's location in the raster is identified by row and column coordinates. By assigning a value to each cell, the corresponding attribute data for that location are also stored. The end result of this conversion process is a set of cells, each with a specified location and an attribute value. These data can then be entered into a computer-compatible file and stored in the GIS database.

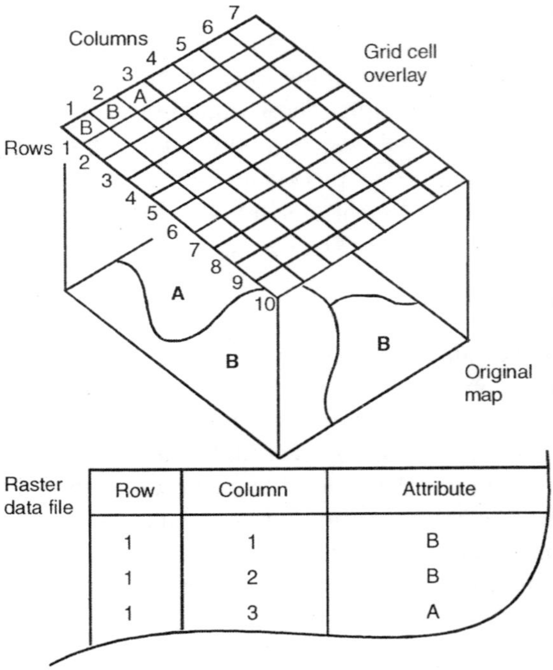

Figure 1.5. A raster model stores spatial and attribute data together for sets of grid cells registered to the original map. The location of each grid cell is defined by row and column coordinates with an associated attribute tag linked to each cell. The end result of converting a map to a raster data file is a GIS-compatible digital data file.

Perhaps the most critical issue in using a raster GIS is the selection of an appropriate grid cell size. The user is forced to examine the trade-off between data resolution (how small grid cells are in the raster array) and storage requirements (increasing the number of rows and columns causes exponential increases in storage requirements). The use of smaller cells records greater detail in the GIS, so the user would normally attempt to select the smallest practical cell size. The choice of cell size depends on many factors, including the resolution of the original map data, the degree of resolution needed in the GIS analysis, the time and money available for data compilation, available storage space on the GIS computer, and cell sizes already employed for previously existing raster data that the user may want to incorporate into the GIS database.

Cell size is critical because it is one of the base map parameters that must be standard for all of the layers in a raster GIS. While it is technically feasible to store data at different cell sizes, all analysis and multi-map manipulation operations require that cell sizes be the same (as well as projection, scale, and coordinate system). Typically, a GIS allows the user to adjust cell sizes within the database. The user must be aware of the nature of the data and not violate the limits of those data. For example, when attempting to combine two data layers that have been compiled and stored at two cell sizes, the user must increase the cell size on the layer having smaller cells to match that of the layer using larger cells. For this reason, the highest level of detail stored in such a database is only equal to the map layer having the largest cell size. This cell size becomes, in essence, the lowest common geography for the raster-based GIS.

Vector

A vector data structure is very different from a raster data model. Whereas the raster data model uses sets of grid cells to record all data, a vector model stores all spatial data as either a point, line, or polygon. These three types of spatial data are referred to as features, and a vector GIS can be termed a "feature-based technology." Figure 1.6 shows an example of a vector data model. When a vector model represents an entity as a point (e.g., a well), a single coordinate pair is used to specify its location. A feature represented as a line (e.g., a stream) uses a linked set of coordinates, and a feature represented as a polygon, which is an alternative form of a line (e.g., a lake), must have the same beginning and ending point coordinates. In a raster model, a point is a single cell, a line is a linked set of cells, and a polygon is a group or neighborhood of similarly encoded cells. For all three types of features stored in a vector GIS, an attribute code is entered into the GIS files to identify the object. For example, a lake would be vectorized (added to the database as a vector map) as a polygon by storing the linked set of coordinates for the shoreline and the attribute code "lake" would be entered in the GIS files to identify that group of cells.

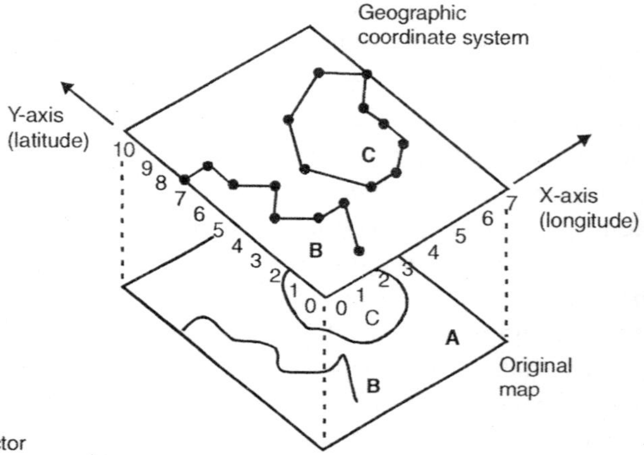

Vector data file

Entity	X, Y Coordinates	Name
A	5, 1	Well
B	0,7; 1,7; 1,6; 2,5; 1,4; 2,3; 3,3; 2,1	stream
C	4,3; 5,3; 6,4; 6,5; 6,6; 7,7; 6,8; 4,7; 3,5; 4,3	lake

Figure 1.6. A vector model stores all spatial data as primitive features or points, lines, and polygons. Points are stored as discrete coordinate pairs, lines as linked sets of coordinates, and polygons as areas with an alternative form of a line that has the same beginning and ending coordinates. Attribute tags such as "lake" are then added to the spatial data file. The end result of converting a map to a vector data file is a GIS-compatible digital data file.

Advantages of Digitized Storage

Whether a GIS is raster- or vector-based, spatial data from map manuscripts must be compiled and stored in a simplified form that the computer can recognize. Each of these models handles spatial and attribute data in such a way as to allow the digital processing capability of a computer to be applied to managing and storing data. Computers cannot store maps in their original form; they must be converted via a digitizing process. That digitizing and storage process often is a time-consuming and expensive part of building a GIS; the cost of initially digitizing all data may comprise a majority of the total cost of system implementation. Despite the cost, digital maps stored on a computer are in a much more dynamic form and can be easily and rapidly processed. Digital data can also be exchanged between GIS systems, copies can easily be made and distributed to multiple users, and data can be shared using telecommunications options available to modern computer users. Thus, the end result of converting data into GIS-compatible format is a more dynamic, flexible data environment.

Manipulation

Once data are stored in a GIS, many retrieval, analysis, and output options are available to users. These functions are often available in the form of "toolkits." A toolkit is a set of generic functions that a GIS user can employ to manipulate and analyze geographic data. Toolkits provide processing functions such as data retrieval, measuring area and perimeter, overlaying maps, performing map algebra, and reclassifying map data. A GIS usually includes a basic set of computer programs or "tools." The functions provided by the toolkit vary with the software package. A companion piece, *Introduction to Data Analysis Using Geographic Information Systems* (Falbo et al. 1991), describes analysis functions in detail.

Output

The final functional task of a GIS is to generate output; usually a map. GIS-generated maps are compiled from the many data sets contained in the digital GIS and match exact user specifications. Map output may employ several color and symbology schemes, and will be sized and scaled to meet user needs. These output products resemble hand-drafted maps and fulfill essentially the same purposes. However, it is incorrect to refer to GIS simply as a mapping system. Although GIS is able to generate high-quality map output, its ability to perform analysis and management sets it apart from the more limited computer-mapping packages.

Another form of output from a GIS is tabular or report information. Data summarized according to user-defined classes or within user-defined areas can readily be generated in a textual format. This output may also be routed to another computer application such as a statistical analysis package or a graphing package for subsequent analysis and display.

The digital data themselves are often overlooked as a type of GIS output. Data files can be readily shared between users or systems. Because the data are in a digital format they can easily be copied, transmitted via cable or phone line, or distributed on media such as diskettes, computer-compatible tapes, or optical media such as compact disks. This greatly facilitates data sharing and provides increased access to data and information across the entire user spectrum.

Having completed a review of the basic elements and functions of a GIS, you can understand what GIS is designed to do. A few of the relative advantages and disadvantages of a GIS approach can now be assessed from a foundation of understanding. On that basis, the next section examines a generic approach to getting started with GIS.

Planning for GIS

Many different types of organizations and users are interested in getting started with this new and exciting technology. Yet the developers of new GIS projects often find that selecting and implementing a GIS solution is a complex and demanding task. In all cases, new and existing GIS users are advised to engage in a strategic planning process prior to system acquisition, start-up, or the initiation of a new project on an existing system. Private consultants and vendors can assist with the planning process. It is also recommended that organizations planning to adopt GIS discuss the utility of the technology with existing GIS users who are performing similar tasks.

The concept of a strategic process is diagrammed in Figure 1.7. This process is compatible with the data-centered approaches outlined in Components of GIS and Functions of GIS, and follows a common-sense approach to getting started.

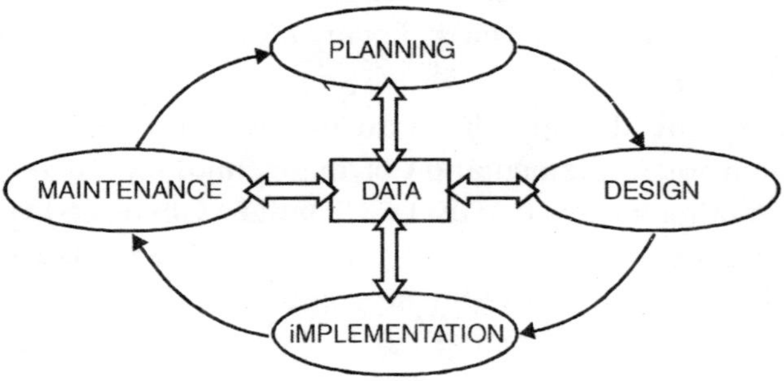

Figure 1.7. The concept of a GIS life cycle is useful for understanding a strategic approach to getting started with GIS. Users maintain a data-centered approach while designing and implementing a GIS solution that is based on a systematic evaluation of needs as surveyed during the initial planning phase. Implementation is often incremental and follows a pilot project or prototype used to examine the feasibility of a GIS for the purpose at hand. GIS systems as well as data require ongoing commitments in order to meet the GIS design goals and to maintain data that have full utility.

Phase 1—Planning

A planning process is the first stage in the life cycle. This phase involves a systematic review of users, their data, and their information needs. This is the time to educate decision makers about the costs and benefits of GIS and to include potential users in the planning process so that they receive an overview of the technology. Once a thorough understanding of user needs is established, the second life cycle phase, system design, can begin.

Phase 2—System Design

The design phase matches user needs to GIS functionality. Design includes not only selection of hardware and software, but also the design of the GIS spatial and attribute database. Part of that database design will include base map specifications for scale, projection, and coordinate systems. Data should be tracked using a "data dictionary." A data dictionary catalogs all data entered into the integrated GIS database and maintains current records on the source, accuracy, the time of data collection, and overall nature of each and every data element stored in the GIS. Establishment and maintenance of a robust data dictionary are essential to the overall utility of any GIS.

During the design phase an incremental plan is often anticipated for implementation of the technology. Incremental implementation means that users will build a GIS piece-by-piece. Oftentimes a prototype or pilot project is implemented so that lessons learned can be used to streamline the development of a fully-implemented system.

Phase 3—Implementation

During the implementation phase, attention to all user needs must be provided through training and education. Hands-on users must be trained to utilize and maintain the system and the database. All types of users should be made cognizant of how the GIS will affect them and their data processing tasks. They must also be made aware of the changes that GIS will introduce in the area of information generation and decision making.

Phase 4—Maintenance

Finally, a GIS application must be maintained and kept current in terms of data and user support. In some cases, a GIS is designed to meet the needs of a specific, finite project. In other instances, GIS is used to support an on-going mission or program. In the former case, the GIS application will terminate once the project is completed and maintenance will probably not be an issue. However, even if the initial GIS application is no longer being utilized, the data generated for the initial project may be useful to other projects or users. In those instances, a current data dictionary will be vital for determining the utility of the existing digital data for other uses.

In the case of an on-going GIS effort the system must be kept up-to-date in order to fulfill its design goals. Maintenance includes updating hardware and software, adding new data and updating existing data records, and keeping users current in terms of system functionality.

Implications of GIS

In any situation where it is applied, GIS may fundamentally change the way spatial data are managed and analyzed. When potential users are unaware of how GIS will affect them and their duties, the changes may be disturbing. GIS developers have a responsibility to initiate and maintain a focus on user issues and concerns. Ultimately, the success of a GIS venture is determined by the ability of the system to fulfill design goals. Those design goals are determined in the planning phase of the system life cycle, during which an understanding of data issues and user needs must be paramount. Potential users must be made cognizant of the role that GIS will play in their jobs, and should know that the responsibility for the success of the GIS effort ultimately resides on how well the system responds to their needs and demands.

An organization adopting GIS will need to make adjustments in user access to, and control of, information. Because of the dynamic nature of GIS, it is often difficult to track data and maintain up-to-date records on data status. Data can be copied, shared, and modified with ease in automated systems. Not all data transactions can be monitored; user access must often be restricted so that the integrity of the system is not jeopardized. Indeed, system security is a significant issue, particularly in a networked computing environment. A current data dictionary is very helpful in monitoring data integrity.

The organization must also adapt to changes in the cost of information. Because GIS requires such a strict structuring of spatial and attribute data, system developers and users must be prepared to deal with the overhead costs associated with a GIS approach. As mentioned previously, the process of converting existing mapped data into a computer-compatible format is time-consuming and costly. Conversely, a very robust data environment can be established via GIS when proper stipulations and standards are imposed on data development and use. In a GIS, data can be shared efficiently and effectively, and formerly diverse and incompatible databases can be integrated.

The GIS that results from development efforts is ultimately only as good as the data contained in the system. A GIS will not fundamentally change the nature of spatial and attribute data, nor will it correct basic inaccuracies in data. GIS provides a rigorous structure for spatial and attribute data, but bad or incorrect data of both types can be made to fit a base map standard. The bottom line is, just because data are in a GIS does not mean that they are correct.

Users should be made aware of the limitations of the GIS approach. For example, a typical GIS can technically adjust the scale of any map to user specifications. It is up to the user not to violate the precision of the data, even if the software will allow this function to be performed. For example, if data are mapped at a relatively small scale of 1:250,000, the user must decide if rescaling the map to a larger scale of 1:15,840 presumes more precision or accuracy than really exists in the data.

The powerful output capabilities afforded by GIS in producing maps or reports on paper or as displays on computer monitors provide unparalleled opportunities for visualizing spatial data. Users who generate these products must exercise care in presenting information accurately and honestly. Persons who produce information from a GIS should be aware of the intended audience and the type of information that needs to be communicated. Similarly, users of GIS output should exercise care in interpreting and drawing conclusions from those information products. In every case, knowing something about the data is critical to proper and complete use of GIS output.

Conclusion

GIS has been defined as a computerized system for compiling, storing, manipulating, and outputting spatial data. A true GIS was shown to comprise data, hardware, software, and users. A good way to analyze the GIS approach is to focus on the spatial data that is handled by the GIS.

A GIS provides a hybrid database that contains both spatial and attribute data. Spatial data describe the location of objects with respect to a known coordinate system, while attribute data describe the nature or characteristics of spatial phenomena. Data flow through a GIS via a series of system functions. Data can be manipulated in a GIS using a series of functional programs called "tools" that operate on mapped data. Users also can elect a series of output options for communicating the results of their analyses to end users.

Getting started with GIS can be a daunting task. Although the concept of a GIS as a stacked series of map data layers is quite intuitive, the actual development of a useful system demands much from system developers. As a GIS automates or computerizes traditional mapped data, the GIS user must bear the costs associated with data compilation. GIS requires that data be tied to common geographic parameters or rules called a "base map." System developers should follow a life cycle approach to establishing GIS projects or applications, which is a strategic approach that follows through on planning, designing, implementing, and maintaining these types of systems. A life cycle approach explicitly considers users' needs and also focuses on the data that must be managed and analyzed by the system.

GIS will cause profound changes in the way we collect, store, analyze, and share geographic data. Many of these changes are predictable and their impacts can be estimated before the change actually occurs. In some instances, pilot or prototype projects will be conducted to test the feasibility of a GIS solution. Users of GIS can rely on the experiences of other users and organizations as well as advice from private consultants to help them through the start-up phases of a GIS effort. Ultimately, each GIS is unique; its data, users, and applications must be tailored to fit the demands of its users.

2

History of GIS

Introduction

The earliest use of the geographic method, in 1854 John Snow depicted a cholera outbreak in London using points to represent the locations of some individual cases. His study of the distribution of cholera led to the source of the disease, a contaminated water pump within the heart of the cholera outbreak.

While the basic elements of topology and theme existed previously in cartography, the John Snow map was unique, using cartographic methods, not only to depict but also to analyze, clusters of geographically dependent phenomena for the first time.

The early 20th century saw the development of "photo lithography" where maps were separated into layers. Computer hardware development spurred by nuclear weapon research would lead to general purpose computer "mapping" applications by the early 1960s.

The year 1962 saw the development of the world's first true operational GIS in Ottawa, Ontario, Canada by the federal Department of Forestry and Rural Development. Developed by Dr. Roger Tomlinson, it was called the "Canada Geographic Information System" (CGIS) and was used to store, analyze, and manipulate data collected for the Canada Land Inventory (CLI) an initiative to determine the land capability for rural Canada by mapping information about soils, agriculture, recreation, wildlife, waterfowl, forestry, and land use at a scale of 1:50,000. A rating classification factor was also added to permit analysis.

CGIS was the world's first "system" and was an improvement over "mapping" applications as it provided capabilities for overlay, measurement, and digitizing/scanning. It supported a national coordinate system that spanned the continent, coded lines as "arcs" having a true embedded topology, and it stored the attribute and locational information in separate files. As a result of this, Tomlinson has become known as the "father of GIS," particularly for his use of overlays in promoting the spatial analysis of convergent geographic data. CGIS lasted into the 1990s and built the largest digital land resource database in Canada. It was developed as a mainframe based system in support of federal and provincial resource planning and management. Its strength was continent-wide analysis of complex data sets. The CGIS was never available in a commercial form.

In 1964, Howard T Fisher formed the Laboratory for Computer Graphics and Spatial Analysis at the Harvard Graduate School of Design (LCGSA 1965-1991), where a number of important theoretical concepts in spatial data handling were developed, and which by the 1970s had distributed seminal software code and systems, such as 'SYMAP', 'GRID', and 'ODYSSEY' which served as literal and inspirational sources for subsequent commercial development to universities, research centers, and corporations worldwide.

By the early 1980s, M&S Computing (later Intergraph), Environmental Systems Research Institute (ESRI) and CARIS emerged as commercial vendors of GIS software, successfully incorporating many of the CGIS features, combining the first generation approach to separation of spatial and attribute information with a second generation approach to organizing attribute data into database structures. In parallel, the development of a public domain GIS was begun in 1982 by the U.S. Army Corp of Engineering Research Laboratory (USA-CERL) in Champaign, Illinois, a branch of the U.S. Army Corps of Engineers to meet the need of the United States military for software for land management and environmental planning. The later 1980s and 1990s industry growth were spurred on by the growing use of GIS on Unix workstations and the personal computer. By the end of the 20th century, the rapid growth in various systems had been consolidated and standardized on relatively few platforms and users were beginning to export the concept of viewing GIS data over the Internet, requiring data format and transfer standards. More recently, there is a growing number of free, open source GIS packages which run on a range of operating systems and can be customized to perform specific tasks.

Techniques used in GIS

Data creation

Modern GIS technologies use digital information, for which various digitized data creation methods are used. The most common method of data creation is digitization, where a hard copy map or survey plan is transferred into a digital medium through the use of a computer-aided design (CAD) program, and geo-referencing capabilities. With the wide availability of ortho-rectified imagery (both from satellite and aerial sources), heads-up digitizing is becoming the main avenue through which geographic data is extracted. Heads-up digitizing involves the tracing of geographic data directly on top of the aerial imagery instead of through the traditional method of tracing the geographic form on a separate digitizing tablet.

Relating information from different sources

If you could relate information about the rainfall of your state to aerial photographs of your county, you might be able to tell which wetlands dry up at certain times of the year. A GIS, which can use information from many different sources in many different forms, can help with such analyses. The primary requirement for the source data consists of knowing the locations for the variables. Location may be annotated by x, y, and z coordinates of longitude, latitude, and elevation, or by other geocode systems like ZIP Codes or by highway mile markers. Any variable that can be located spatially can be fed into a GIS. Several computer databases that can be directly entered into a GIS are being produced by government agencies and non-government organizations. Different kinds of data in map form can be entered into a GIS.

A GIS can also convert existing digital information, which may not yet be in map form, into forms it can recognize and use. For example, digital satellite images generated through remote sensing can be analyzed to produce a map-like layer of digital information about vegetative covers. Another fairly developed resource for naming GIS objects is the Getty Thesaurus of Geographic Names (GTGN), which is a structured vocabulary containing around 1,000,000 names and other information about places. Likewise, census or hydrologic tabular data can be converted to map-like form, serving as layers of thematic information in a GIS.

Data representation

GIS data represents real world objects (roads, land use, elevation) with digital data. Real world objects can be divided into two abstractions: discrete objects (a house) and continuous fields (rain fall amount or elevation). There are two broad methods used to store data in a GIS for both abstractions: Raster and Vector.

Raster data type consists of rows and columns of cells where in each cell is stored a single value. Raster data can be images (raster images) with each pixel (or cell) containing a color value. Additional values recorded for each cell may be a discrete value, such as land use, a continuous value, such as temperature, or a null value if no data is available. While a raster cell stores a single value, it can be extended by using raster bands to represent RGB (red, green, blue) colors, colormaps (a mapping between a thematic code and RGB value), or an extended attribute table with one row for each unique cell value. The resolution of the raster data set is its cell width in ground units.

Raster data is stored in various formats; from a standard file-based structure of TIF, JPEG, etc. to binary large object (BLOB) data stored directly in a relational database management system (RDBMS) similar to other vector-based feature classes. Database storage, when properly indexed, typically allows for quicker retrieval of the raster data but can require storage of millions of significantly-sized records.

Vector

Vector data type uses geometries such as points, lines (series of point coordinates), or polygons, also called areas (shapes bounded by lines), to represent objects. Examples include property boundaries for a housing subdivision represented as polygons and well locations represented as points. Vector features can be made to respect spatial integrity through the application of topology rules such as 'polygons must not overlap'. Vector data can also be used to represent continuously varying phenomena. Contour lines and triangulated irregular networks (TIN) are used to represent elevation or other continuously changing values. TINs record values at point locations, which are connected by lines to form an irregular mesh of triangles. The face of the triangles represent the terrain surface.

Advantages and Disadvantages

There are advantages and disadvantages to using a raster or vector data model to represent reality. Raster data sets record a value for all points in the area covered which may require more storage space than representing data in a vector format that can store data only where needed. Raster data also allows easy implementation of overlay operations, which are more difficult with vector data. Vector data can be displayed as vector graphics used on traditional maps, whereas raster data will appear as an image that may have a blocky appearance for object boundaries. Vector data can be easier to register, scale, and re-project. This can simplify combining vector layers from different sources. Vector data are more compatible with relational database environment. They can be part of a relational table as a normal column and processes using a multitude of operators.

Voxel

Selected GIS additionally support the voxel data model. A voxel (a portmanteau of the words *volumetric* and *pixel*) is a volume element, representing a value on a regular grid in three dimensional space. This is analogous to a pixel, which represents 2D image data. Voxels can be interpolated from 3D point clouds (3D point vector data), or merged from 2D raster slices.

Non-spatial data

Additional non-spatial data can also be stored besides the spatial data represented by the coordinates of a vector geometry or the position of a raster cell. In vector data, the additional data are attributes of the object. For example, a forest inventory polygon may also have an identifier value and information about tree species. In raster data the cell value can store attribute information, but it can also be used as an identifier that can relate to records in another table.

Data Capture

Data capture – entering information into the system – consumes much of the time of GIS practitioners. There are a variety of methods used to enter data into a GIS where it is stored in a digital format.

Existing data printed on paper or PET film maps can be digitized or scanned to produce digital data. A digitizer produces vector data as an operator traces points, lines, and polygon boundaries from a map. Scanning a map results in raster data that could be further processed to produce vector data.

Survey data can be directly entered into a GIS from digital data collection systems on survey instruments. Positions from a Global Positioning System (GPS), another survey tool, can also be directly entered into a GIS.

Remotely sensed data also plays an important role in data collection and consist of sensors attached to a platform. Sensors include cameras, digital scanners and LIDAR, while platforms usually consist of aircraft and satellites.

The majority of digital data currently comes from photo interpretation of aerial photographs. Soft copy workstations are used to digitize features directly from stereo pairs of digital photographs. These systems allow data to be captured in 2 and 3 dimensions, with elevations measured directly from a stereo pair using principles of photogrammetry. Currently, analog aerial photos are scanned before being entered into a soft copy system, but as high quality digital cameras become cheaper this step will be skipped.

Satellite remote sensing provides another important source of spatial data. Here satellites use different sensor packages to passively measure the reflectance from parts of the electromagnetic spectrum or radio waves that were sent out from an active sensor such as radar. Remote sensing collects raster data that can be further processed to identify objects and classes of interest, such as land cover.

When data is captured, the user should consider if the data should be captured with either a relative accuracy or absolute accuracy, since this could not only influence how information will be interpreted but also the cost of data capture.

In addition to collecting and entering spatial data, attribute data is also entered into a GIS. For vector data, this includes additional information about the objects represented in the system.

After entering data into a GIS, the data usually requires editing, to remove errors, or further processing. For vector data it must be made "topologically correct" before it can be used for some advanced analysis. For example, in a road network, lines must connect with nodes at an intersection. Errors such as undershoots and overshoots must also be removed. For scanned maps, blemishes on the source map may need to be removed from the resulting raster. For example, a fleck of dirt might connect two lines that should not be connected.

Raster-to-vector Translation

Data restructuring can be performed by a GIS to convert data into different formats. For example, a GIS may be used to convert a satellite image map to a vector structure by generating lines around all cells with the same classification, while determining the cell spatial relationships, such as adjacency or inclusion.

More advanced data processing can occur with image processing, a technique developed in the late 1960s by NASA and the private sector to provide contrast enhancement, false colour rendering and a variety of other techniques including use of two dimensional Fourier transforms.

Since digital data are collected and stored in various ways, the two data sources may not be entirely compatible. So a GIS must be able to convert geographic data from one structure to another.

Projections, Coordinate Systems and Registration

A property ownership map and a soils map might show data at different scales. Map information in a GIS must be manipulated so that it registers, or fits, with information gathered from other maps. Before the digital data can be analyzed, they may have to undergo other manipulations projection and coordinate conversions, for example that integrate them into a GIS.

The earth can be represented by various models, each of which may provide a different set of coordinates (e.g., latitude, longitude, elevation) for any given point on the earth's surface. The simplest model is to assume the earth is a perfect sphere. As more measurements of the earth have accumulated, the models of the earth have become more sophisticated and more accurate. In fact, there are models that apply to different areas of the earth to provide increased accuracy (e.g., North American Datum, 1927 - NAD27 - works well in North America, but not in Europe).

Projection is a fundamental component of map making. A projection is a mathematical means of transferring information from a model of the Earth, which represents a three-dimensional curved surface, to a two-dimensional medium paper or a computer screen. Different projections are used for different types of maps because each projection particularly suits certain uses. For example, a projection that accurately represents the shapes of the continents will distort their relative sizes.

Since much of the information in a GIS comes from existing maps, a GIS uses the processing power of the computer to transform digital information, gathered from sources with different projections and/or different coordinate systems, to a common projection and coordinate system. For images, this process is called rectification.

Spatial analysis with GIS

Data modeling

It is difficult to relate wetlands maps to rainfall amounts recorded at different points such as airports, television stations, and high schools. A GIS, however, can be used to depict two- and three-dimensional characteristics of the Earth's surface, subsurface, and atmosphere from information points. For example, a GIS can quickly generate a map with isopleth or contour lines that indicate differing amounts of rainfall.

Such a map can be thought of as a rainfall contour map. Many sophisticated methods can estimate the characteristics of surfaces from a limited number of point measurements. A two-dimensional contour map created from the surface modeling of rainfall point measurements may be overlaid and analyzed with any other map in a GIS covering the same area.

Additionally, from a series of three-dimensional points, or digital elevation model, isopleth lines representing elevation contours can be generated, along with slope analysis, shaded relief, and other elevation products. Watersheds can be easily defined for any given reach, by computing all of the areas contiguous and uphill from any given point of interest. Similarly, an expected thalweg of where surface water would want to travel in intermittent and permanent streams can be computed from elevation data in the GIS.

Topological Modeling

In the past years, were there any gas stations or factories operating next to the swamp? Any within two miles and uphill from the swamp? A GIS can recognize and analyze the spatial relationships that exist within digitally stored spatial data. These topological relationships allow complex spatial modelling and analysis to be performed. Topological relationships between geometric entities traditionally include adjacency (what adjoins what), containment (what encloses what), and proximity (how close something is to something else).

Networks

If all the factories near a wetland were accidentally to release chemicals into the river at the same time, how long would it take for a damaging amount of pollutant to enter the wetland reserve? A GIS can simulate the routing of materials along a linear network. Values such as slope, speed limit, or pipe diameter can be incorporated into network modeling in order to represent the flow of the phenomenon more accurately. Network modelling is commonly employed in transportation planning, hydrology modeling, and infrastructure modeling.

Cartographic Modeling

The term "cartographic modeling" was (probably) coined by Dana Tomlin in his PhD dissertation and later in his book which has the term in the title. Cartographic modeling refers to a process where several thematic layers of the same area are produced, processed, and analyzed. Tomlin used raster layers, but the overlay method (see below) can be used more generally. Operations on map layers can be combined into algorithms, and eventually into simulation or optimization models.

Map Overlay

The combination of two separate spatial data sets (points, lines or polygons) to create a new output vector data set. These overlays are similar to mathematical Venn diagram overlays. A union overlay combines the geographic features and attribute tables of both inputs into a single new output. An intersect overlay defines the area where both inputs overlap and retains a set of attribute fields for each. A symmetric difference overlay defines an output area that includes the total area of both inputs except for the overlapping area.

Data extraction is a GIS process similar to vector overlay, though it can be used in either vector or raster data analysis. Rather than combining the properties and features of both data sets, data extraction involves using a "clip" or "mask" to extract the features of one data set that fall within the spatial extent of another data set.

In raster data analysis, the overlay of data sets is accomplished through a process known as "local operation on multiple rasters" or "map algebra," through a function that combines the values of each raster's matrix. This function may weigh some inputs more than others through use of an "index model" that reflects the influence of various factors upon a geographic phenomenon.

Automated Cartography

Digital cartography and GIS both encode spatial relationships in structured formal representations. GIS is used in digital cartography modeling as a (semi)automated process of making maps, so called Automated Cartography. In practice, it can be a subset of a GIS, within which it is equivalent to the stage of visualization, since in most cases not all of the GIS functionality is used. Cartographic products can be either in a digital or in a hardcopy format. Powerful analysis techniques with different data representation can produce high-quality maps within a short time period. The main problem in Automated Cartography is to use a single set of data to produce multiple products at a variety of scales, a technique known as Generalization.

Geostatistics

Geostatistics is a point-pattern analysis that produces field predictions from data points. It is a way of looking at the statistical properties of those special data. It is different from general applications of statistics because it employs the use of graph theory and matrix algebra to reduce the number of parameters in the data. Only the second-order properties of the GIS data are analyzed.

When phenomena are measured, the observation methods dictate the accuracy of any subsequent analysis. Due to the nature of the data (e.g. traffic patterns in an urban environment; weather patterns over the Pacific Ocean), a constant or dynamic degree of precision is always lost in the measurement. This loss of precision is determined from the scale and distribution of the data collection.

To determine the statistical relevance of the analysis, an average is determined so that points (gradients) outside of any immediate measurement can be included to determine their predicted behavior. This is due to the limitations of the applied statistic and data collection methods, and interpolation is required in order to predict the behavior of particles, points, and locations that are not directly measurable.

Interpolation is the process by which a surface is created, usually a raster data set, through the input of data collected at a number of sample points. There are several forms of interpolation, each which treats the data differently, depending on the properties of the data set. In comparing interpolation methods, the first consideration should be whether or not the source data will change (exact or approximate). Next is whether the method is subjective, a human interpretation, or objective. Then there is the nature of transitions between points: are they abrupt or gradual. Finally, there is whether a method is global (it uses the entire data set to form the model), or local where an algorithm is repeated for a small section of terrain.

Interpolation is a justified measurement because of a Spatial Autocorrelation Principle that recognizes that data collected at any position will have a great similarity to, or influence of those locations within its immediate vicinity.

Digital elevation models (DEM), triangulated irregular networks (TIN), Edge finding algorithms, Theissen Polygons, Fourier analysis, Weighted moving averages, Inverse Distance Weighted, Moving averages, Kriging, Spline, and Trend surface analysis are all mathematical methods to produce interpolative data.

Address Geocoding

Geocoding is calculating spatial locations (X,Y coordinates) from street addresses. A reference theme is required to geocode individual addresses, such as a road centerline file with address ranges. The individual address locations are interpolated, or estimated, by examining address ranges along a road segment. These are usually provided in the form of a table or database. The GIS will then place a dot approximately where that address belongs along the segment of centerline. For example, an address point of 500 will be at the midpoint of a line segment that starts with address 1 and ends with address 1000. Geocoding can also be applied against actual parcel data, typically from municipal tax maps. In this case, the result of the geocoding will be an actually positioned space as opposed to an interpolated point.

It should be noted that there are several (potentially dangerous) caveats that are often overlooked when using interpolation.

Various algorithms are used to help with address matching when the spellings of addresses differ. Address information that a particular entity or organization has data on, such as the post office, may not entirely match the reference theme. There could be variations in street name spelling, community name, etc. Consequently, the user generally has the ability to make matching criteria more stringent, or to relax those parameters so that more addresses will be mapped. Care must be taken to review the results so as not to erroneously map addresses incorrectly due to overzealous matching parameters.

Reverse Geocoding

Reverse geocoding is the process of returning an estimated street address number as it relates to a given coordinate. For example, a user can click on a road centerline theme (thus providing a coordinate) and have information returned that reflects the estimated house number. This house number is interpolated from a range assigned to that road segment. If the user clicks at the midpoint of a segment that starts with address 1 and ends with 100, the returned value will be somewhere near 50. Note that reverse geocoding does not return actual addresses, only estimates of what should be there based on the predetermined range.

Data Output and Cartography

Cartography is the design and production of maps, or visual representations of spatial data. The vast majority of modern cartography is done with the help of computers, usually using a GIS. Most GIS software gives the user substantial control over the appearance of the data.

Cartographic work serves two major functions:

First, it produces graphics on the screen or on paper that convey the results of analysis to the people who make decisions about resources. Wall maps and other graphics can be generated, allowing the viewer to visualize and thereby understand the results of analyses or simulations of potential events. Web Map Servers facilitate distribution of generated maps through web browsers using various implementations of web-based application programming interfaces (AJAX, Java, Flash, etc).

Second, other database information can be generated for further analysis or use. An example would be a list of all addresses within one mile of a toxic spill.

Graphic Display Techniques

Traditional maps are abstractions of the real world, a sampling of important elements portrayed on a sheet of paper with symbols to represent physical objects. People who use maps must interpret these symbols. Topographic maps show the shape of land surface with contour lines; the actual shape of the land can be seen only in the mind's eye.

Today, graphic display techniques such as shading based on altitude in a GIS can make relationships among map elements visible, heightening one's ability to extract and analyze information. For example, two types of data were combined in a GIS to produce a perspective view of a portion of San Mateo County, California.

- The digital elevation model, consisting of surface elevations recorded on a 30-meter horizontal grid, shows high elevations as white and low elevation as black.
- The accompanying Landsat Thematic Mapper image shows a false-color infrared image looking down at the same area in 30-meter pixels, or picture elements, for the

same coordinate points, pixel by pixel, as the elevation information.

A GIS was used to register and combine the two images to render the three-dimensional perspective view looking down the San Andreas Fault, using the Thematic Mapper image pixels, but shaded using the elevation of the landforms. The GIS display depends on the viewing point of the observer and time of day of the display, to properly render the shadows created by the sun's rays at that latitude, longitude, and time of day.

Spatial ETL

Spatial ETL tools provide the data processing functionality of traditional Extract, Transform, Load (ETL) software, but with a primary focus on the ability to manage spatial data. They provide GIS users with the ability to translate data between different standards and proprietary formats, whilst geometrically transforming the data en-route.

3

GIS Software: Process and Transformation

Introduction

Geographic information can be accessed, transferred, transformed, overlaid, processed and displayed using numerous software applications. Within industry commercial offerings from companies such as ESRI and Mapinfo dominate, offering an entire suite of tools. Government and military departments often use custom software, open source products, such as GRASS, or more specialized products that meet a well defined need. Although free tools exist to view GIS datasets, public access to geographic information is dominated by online resources such as Google Earth and interactive web mapping.

Background

Originally up to the late 1990s, when GIS data was mostly based on large computers and used to maintain internal records, software was a stand-alone product. However with increased access to the internet and networks and demand for distributed geographic data grew, GIS software gradually changed its entire outlook to the delivery of data over a network. GIS software is now usually marketed as combination of various interoperable applications and API's.

Data Creation

GIS processing software is used for the task of preparing data for use within a GIS. This transforms the raw or legacy geographic data into a format usable by GIS products. For example an aerial photograph may need to be stretched (orthorectified) using photogrammetry so that its pixels align with longitude and latitude gradations (or what ever grid is needed). This can be distinguished from the transformations done within GIS analysis software by the fact that these changes are permanent, more complex and time consuming. Thus, a specialized high-end type of software is generally used by a person skilled in Remote Sensing and / or GIS processing aspects of computer science. In addition, AutoCAD, normally used for draughts of engineering projects, can be configured for the editing of vector maps, and has some products that have migrated towards GIS use. It is especially useful as it has strong support for digitization. Raw geographic data can be edited in many standard database and spreadsheet applications and in some cases a text editor may be used as long as care is taken to properly format data.

Comparison of GIS software

Open source software

Most widely used open source applications:

GRASS GIS

GRASS (Geographic Resources Analysis Support System) is an open source, Free Software Geographical information system (GIS) with raster, topological vector, image processing, and graphics production functionality that operates on various platforms through a graphical user interface and shell in the X Window System. It is released under GNU General Public License (GPL).

The recent GRASS 6 release introduces a new topological 2D/ 3D vector engine and support for vector network analysis. Attributes are managed in *.dbf* files or SQL-based DBMS such as MySQL, PostgreSQL/PostGIS, and SQLite. The system is capable of visualizing 3D vector graphics data and voxel volumes. GRASS supports an extensive range of raster and vector formats through the binding to GDAL/OGR libraries, including OGC-conformal

Operating System Support

GIS software	Windows	Mac OS X	Linux	BSD	Unix	Web
CARIS	Yes	No	Yes	Yes	Yes	Yes
Chameleon	Yes	Yes	Yes	Yes	Yes	AMP
ERDAS IMAGINE	Yes	No	No	No	Yes	No
ESRI	Yes	No	Yes	No	Yes	Yes
GeoServer	Yes	Yes	Yes	Yes	Yes	Java
GeoTools	Java	Java	Java	Java	Java	No
GRASS	Yes	Yes	Yes	Yes	Yes	via pyWPS
gvSIG	Java	Java	Java	Java	Java	No
IDRISI	Yes	No	No	No	No	No
ILOG JViews Maps	Java	Java	Java	Java	Java	Java & DHTML/Ajax
ILWIS	Yes	No	No	No	No	No
Intergraph	Yes	No	No	No	CLIX	Yes
JUMP GIS	Java	Java	Java	Java	Java	No
LandSerf	Java	Java	Java	Java	Java	No
Manifold System	Yes	No	No	No	No	Yes
MapInfo	Yes	No	Yes	No	Yes	Yes
MapServer	Yes	Yes	Yes	Yes	Yes	AMP
Maptitude	Yes	No	No	No	No	Yes
MapWindow GIS	Yes (ActiveX)	No	No	No	No	No
Oracle Spatial	Yes	Yes	Yes	No	Yes	Yes

GIS software	Windows	Mac OS X	Linux	BSD	Unix	Web
Panorama	"GIS Map 2005"	No	"GIS Panorama"	No	No	No
PostGIS	Yes	Yes	Yes	Yes	Yes	Yes
Quantum GIS	Yes	Yes	Yes	Yes	Yes	Yes
Smallworld	Yes	?	Yes	?	Yes	Yes
SPRING	Yes	No	Yes	No	Solaris	No
TatukGIS	Yes	No	No	No	No	?
TransCAD	Yes	No	No	No	No	Yes
TerraView	Yes	No	Yes	No	No	No
TNTmips	Yes	Yes	Yes	No	Yes	No
TransModeler	Yes	No	No	No	No	No
uDIG	Yes	Yes	Yes	No	No	No
AvisMap GIS Engine	Template:YES	No	No	No	No	Template:DHTML

(Open Geospatial Consortium) Simple Features for interoperability with other GIS. It also supports Linear Reference System.

The GRASS Development Team is a multi-national group consisting of developers at numerous locations. GRASS is one of the eight initial Software Projects of the Open Source Geospatial Foundation.

Architecture

GRASS supports raster and vector data in two and three dimensions. The vector data model is topological, meaning that areas are defined by boundaries and centroids; boundaries cannot overlap within a single layer. This is in contrast with OpenGIS Simple Features, which define vectors more freely, much as a non-georeferenced vector illustration program does.

GRASS is designed as an environment in which tools that perform specific GIS computations are executed. Unlike typical application software, upon starting GRASS, the user is presented with a UNIX shell containing a modified environment that supports the execution of GRASS commands (known as modules). The environment has a state that includes such parameters as the geographic region covered and the map projection in use. All GRASS modules read this state and additionally are given specific parameters (such as input and output maps, or values to use in a computation) when executed. The majority of GRASS modules and capabilities can be operated via a graphical user interface (provided by a GRASS module), as an alternative to manipulating geographic data in shell. There are over 200 core GRASS modules included in the GRASS distribution, and over 100 add-on modules created by users and offered on the GRASS web site. The GRASS libraries and core modules are written in C; other modules are written in C, UNIX shell, Tcl, or other scripting languages. The GRASS modules are designed under the Unix philosophy and hence can be combined using shell scripting to create more complex or specialized modules by a user without knowledge of C programming.

There is cooperation between GRASS and Quantum GIS (QGIS). Recent versions of QGIS can be executed within the GRASS environment, allowing QGIS to be used as a user-friendly graphical interface to GRASS that more closely resembles other graphical GIS software than does the unique shell-based GRASS interface.

History

GRASS (Geographic Resources Analysis Support System) GRASS has been under continuous development since 1982 and has involved a large number of federal US agencies, universities, and private companies. The core components of GRASS and the management of the integration efforts into GRASS releases were accomplished by the U.S. Army - Construction Engineering Research Laboratory (USA-CERL) in Champaign, Illinois. USA-CERL completed its last release of GRASS as version 4.1 in 1992, and provided five updates and patches to this release through 1995. USA-CERL also wrote the core components of the GRASS 5.0 floating point version.

The development of GRASS was begun by the U.S. Army Corp of Engineering Research Laboratory (USA-CERL) in Champaign, Illinois, a branch of the U.S. Army Corps of Engineers to meet the need of the United States military for software for land management and environmental planning. An key motivation was the National Environmental Policy Act. The development platform was UNIX running on VAX hardware. During 1982 through 1995, USA-CERL led the development of GRASS, with the involvement of numerous others, including universities and other federal agencies. USA-CERL officially ceased its involvement in GRASS after release 4.1, though development had been limited to minor patches since 1993. A group formed at Baylor University to take over the software, releasing GRASS 4.2. Around this period, the license of the originally public-domain GRASS software was changed to the GNU GPL and a port of the software to Linux was made. In 1998, Markus Neteler, the current project leader, announced the release of GRASS 4.2.1, which offered major improvements including a new graphical user interface.

Subsequently, GRASS has evolved into a powerful software suite with a wide range of applications in many different areas of scientific research. GRASS is currently used in academic and commercial settings around the world, as well as many governmental agencies including NASA, NOAA, USDA, DLR, CSIRO, the National Park Service, the U.S. Census Bureau, USGS, and many environmental consulting companies.

GRASS development is split into a stable branch (6.2) and a development branch (6.3). The stable branch is recommended for most users, while the 6.3 branch operates as a testbed for new features.

MapServer

MapServer is an open source internet map server, which runs as a CGI program. MapServer was developed by the University of Minnesota. MapServer was originally developed with support from NASA, which needed a way to make its satellite imagery available to the public.

Technical

MapServer supports Open Geospatial Consortium (OGC) standards, including Web Map Service (WMS) and Web Feature Service (WFS). MapServer works with PostgreSQL and its PostGIS extension, and supports proprietary GIS formats including ESRI's Shapefile format. MapServer uses OGR and GDAL libraries to translate files from one file format to another. MapServer supports PHP, Python, Perl, Ruby, Java, and C# for scripting and customization.

Open Source Geospatial Foundation

In November 2005, Autodesk, the MapServer Technical Steering Committee Members, the University of Minnesota, and DM Solutions Group announced the creation of the MapServer Foundation. With this announcement, Autodesk announced that its internet mapping application, MapGuide, would be developed as an open source application with all new code and be named "MapServer Enterprise". The existing MapServer application would be renamed "MapServer Cheetah". This name change was overwhelmingly opposed by the MapServer community. Autodesk then backed off this name change and retained the name, "MapGuide" for its product. Also, plans to establish the MapServer Foundation were scrapped; Instead, the Open Source Geospatial Foundation (OsGeo) was established to include MapServer and other open source GIS projects.

Other open source GIS applications:

Chameleon (GIS)

Chameleon is an open source, distributed, highly configurable, environment for developing Web Mapping applications. It is built on MapServer as the core mapping engine and works with all MapServer supported data formats. It also works well with OpenGIS Consortium standards for Web Map Services WMS and WMT Viewer Contexts through MapServer's support for these standards.

Chameleon has a plugin architecture. A large number of plugins, or widgets as they are called by the Chameleon developers, are available. A Chameleon widget can implement a mapping task such as zooming, panning, showing legends, or displaying map coordinates. Over a hundred widgets are distributed with the application and developers can easily create their own widget for any specific task.

Chameleon is written in the PHP scripting language with snippets of Javascript code to handle browser functionality. The latest version as of September 10, 2006 was v2.4.1

gvSIG

gvSIG is a multilingual, open source geographic information system (GIS) that can handle both vector and raster data. It features basic editing tools for the creation and maintenance of vector or raster spatial data on a variety of file formats, including remote data sources. gvSIG is being actively developed in Java by IVER Tecnologías under the GNU General Public License (GPL). Its name is a Catalan abbreviation that stands for *Generalitat Valenciana, Sistema d'Informació Geogràfica*.

gvSIG was started in 2003 when the *Conselleria d'Infraestructures i Transports* (CIT) of Valencian Country proposed the development of software for the management of geographic information. The private enterprise IVER Tecnologías won the proposal and is now developing the software together with the Generalitat Valenciana and the Jaume I University of Castellon.

Currently gvSIG runs on Windows, Linux, and Mac OS X operating systems. It supports many open and proprietary standards of geospatial data. A plugin system allows for expandability and compliance with many standards of the Open Geospatial Consortium (OGC) making it compatible with many other GIS software and data.

Standards

gvSIG supports the following data formats:

- Vector formats: shapefile, DXF, DGN, DWG
- Raster formats: ECW, MrSID, JPEG, jp2, TIFF, geoTIFF, PNG, GIF

gvSIG is able to read remote data with Open Geospatial Consortium (OGC) standards:

- Web Map Service (WMS)
- Web Feature Service (WFS)
- Web Coverage Service (WCS)

gvSIG also offers support for remote data from ESRI's ArcIMS.

The WMS has been tested with MapServer, DeeGree and GeoServer; the WCS with MapServer; and the WFS with MapServer and GeoServer.

There are plugins available that enable gvSIG to read ERDAS IMG files and also connect to PostGIS and MySQL databases.

ILWIS

ILWIS (Integrated Land and Water Information System) is a GIS / Remote sensing software that integrates image, vector and thematic data. ILWIS features include digitizing, editing, analysis and display of data as well as production of quality maps.

ILWIS was initially developed and distributed by ITC Enschede (International Institute for Geo-Information Science and Earth Observation) in the Netherlands as shareware, but since 1 July 2007 it is distributed under the terms of the GNU General Public License and is thus free software. The current version is ILWIS 3.4 Open.

Though lagging behind other similar commercial software in a number of functionalities, ILWIS is expected to improve as open source software. Similar to the GRASS GIS in many respects, ILWIS is however presently available natively only on Microsoft Windows.

Features

ILWIS uses GIS techniques that integrate image processing capabilities, a tabular database and conventional GIS characteristics. The major features include:

- Integrated raster and vector design
- On-screen and tablet digitizing

- Comprehensive set of image processing tools
- Orthophoto, image georeferencing, transformation and mosaicing
- Advanced modeling and spatial data analysis
- 3D visualization with interactive editing for optimal view findings
- Rich projection and coordinate system library
- Geostatistical analyses, with Kriging for improved interpolation
- Import and export using the GDAL library
- Advanced data management
- WYSIWYG Layout editor to position annotation and multiple map views on scale
- Advanced Data Storage
- Stereoscopy tools - To create a stereo pair from two aerial photographs
- Transparency to display raster and polygon maps
- Pyramid layers for fast display of large raster maps
- ADO/ODBC to access databases
- Hydrologic Flow Operations
- GARtrip import - Map Import allows the import of GARtrip Text files with GPS data
- Spatial Multiple Criteria Evaluation (SMCE)
- DEM operations
- Variable Threshold Computation, to help preparing a threshold map for drainage network extraction
- Horton Statistics, to calculate the number of streams, the average stream length, the average area of catchments for Strahler stream orders
- Georeference editors

Applications

Applications in Earth Sciences

Applied geomorphology and Natural hazards

- Hazard, vulnerability and risk analysis
- Flood hazard analysis

- Modelling cyclone hazards
- Modelling erosion
- Statistical landslide hazard analysis
- Deterministic landslide hazard zonation
- Seismic landslide hazard zonation
- Coal fire hazard management
- Accident risk analysis on roads

Engineering Geology

- Creating an engineering geological data base

Surface hydrology

- Watershed area management studies
- Irrigation water requirement
- Irrigation area characteristics
- Determination of peak runoff
- Morgan approach for erosion modelling

Hydro geology

- Artificial recharge studies
- Assessing aquifer vulnerability to pollution

Geology

- Remote sensing and GIS techniques applied to geological survey
- Geological data integration

Applications in Environmental Management

Neighborhood modelling

- Modelling with neighbourhood operators
- Extracting topographic and terrain variables for distributed models

Data combination

- Tools for map analysis applied to the selection of a waste disposal site

Soil pollution management

- Environmental chemistry of contaminated soils

Land Resource and Urban Surveys

Urban surveys

- Updating a land use map with oblique air photos
- Analysis of urban change and spatial pattern
- Analysis of suitability for urban expansion

Land use planning

- Analysing the fuelwood demand
- Vegetation cover studies
- Land resource management
- Regional economic planning

Soil surveys

- Soil micromorphology analysis
- Soil erosion modelling

Global radiation studies

- Solar radiation mapping

Application in Cartography

- Cartography
- Layer tinting and shading

Other Applications

- Biodiversity studies

Criticisms

ILWIS though has very good GIS analysis modules, lacks the user friendliness in certain areas. For example, drawing a polygon is not straight forward action, but requires drawing of lines and then going through a quirky procedure called *polygonizing*. Importing through PCI's GeoGateway being a proprietary component has been removed in version 3.4 open and the available GDAL library is not well integrated.

JUMP GIS

Features

- a Java based GIS and programming framework, platform independent (Windows, Linux, Unix, Macintosh)

- reads and writes ESRI SHP, GML files, DXF and PostGIS (with PlugIns)
- full geometry and attribute editing
- OpenGIS SFS compliant
- Geometry algorithms based on Java Topology Suite
- a lot of third party plugins exists (e.g connecting to Postgis database or ArcSDE, Raster files - e.g. tiff)
- easy extensible GIS programming environment for own GIS-applications
- supports a couple of languages (EN, FR, DE, ES, PT)
- free of costs
- OpenSource licence: GPL

The Beginning of JUMP an OpenSource GIS

In 2002, as a project for the British Columbia Ministry of Sustainable Resource Management, Vivid Solutions Inc. created a software program to do automated matching ("conflation") of roads and rivers from different digital maps. The software team wisely made the program flexible enough to be used not just for roads and rivers, but almost any kind of spatial data: provincial boundaries, power-station locations, satellite images, and so on. The program was named JUMP (JAVA Unified Mapping Platform), and it has become a popular, free Geographic Information System (GIS).

Why JUMP was left behind and OpenJUMP arose

After the initial creation and deployment of JUMP, regular development of the program by Vivid Solutions stopped. However, the company was gracious enough to continue offering support to the user community that had grown around JUMP, and answering the questions of developers that had begun to improve JUMP in small ways, or who had customized it to fit their needs. Martin Davis and Jon Aquino, two former employees of Vivid Solutions that worked on the original JUMP, were valuable resources who played a key role in the growth of this community centered around JUMP.

It soon became evident that both the users and developers would benefit from a "unified" JUMP platform. This central or core platform would eliminate the compatibility issues that plagued the JUMP user community, and would give developers a platform on which to focus and coordinate their efforts. A number of the lead members from each team working with JUMP formed the JPP Development Committee, whose purpose was to guide and oversee this new unified platform. A name was chosen for this open source GIS program to be based on JUMP, "OpenJUMP".

File Formats

One important feature of Jump and OpenJUMP is the abililty to work with GIS data in GML format. GML or "Geography Markup Language" is an "xml" (text-based) format for GIS data. It is a way to describe spatial information in a human readable form, and is an accepted "open standard" for GIS data.

OpenJUMP can currently read and write GML data, and the team hopes to develop a number of utilities that will improve OpenJUMP's ability to work with GML.

The ability to work with an open format like GML so important to some implementors because it gives alternatives to proprietary formats like Autodesk DWG files or ESRI Shapefiles.

OpenJUMP nevertheless also reads and writes ESRI Shapefiles and supports ESRI ASCII grid format with an OpenJump plugin from the SIGLE team. While OpenJUMP is considered primarlily a vector based GIS, it also supports rasters, as TIF files or the above ESRI ASCII grid.

MapWindow GIS

MapWindow GIS is an open source GIS (mapping) application and set of programmable mapping components. Because it is distributed as an open source application under the Mozilla Public License distribution license, MapWindow GIS can be reprogrammed to perform different or more specialized tasks. There are also plug-ins available to expand compatibility and functionality. MapWindow GIS is built upon Microsoft .NET technology but is not a multi-platform application and hence does not run on non-Microsoft operating systems including Mac OS X, Linux, and UNIX.

MapWindow GIS is notable software because it has been adopted by the United States Environmental Protection Agency as the primary GIS platform for its BASINS (Better Assessment Science Integrating Point and Nonpoint Sources) watershed analysis and modeling software. BASINS is distributed from the EPA website world-wide and has been used by thousands of watershed modeling professionals at the federal, state, and local level as well as internationally.

MapWindow GIS is continually maintained by an active group of student and voluntary developers who regularly release updates and bug fixes.

PostGIS

PostGIS is an open source geographic information system software program that adds support for geographic objects to the PostgreSQL object-relational database. PostGIS follows the Simple Features for SQL specification from the Open Geospatial Consortium. As such, PostGIS includes:

- Geometry types for points, linestrings, polygons, multipoints, multilinestrings, multipolygons and geometrycollections.
- Spatial predicates for determining the interactions of geometries using the 3x3 Egenhofer matrix.
- Spatial operators for determining geospatial measurements like area, distance, length and perimeter.
- Spatial operators for determining geospatial set operations, like union, difference, symmetric difference and buffers.
- R-tree spatial indexes for high speed spatial querying.
- Index selectivity support, to provide high performance query plans for mixed spatial/non-spatial queries.

The PostGIS implementation is based on "light-weight" geometries and indexes optimized to reduce disk and memory footprint. Using light-weight geometries helps servers increase the amount of data migrated up from physical disk storage into RAM, improving query performance substantially.

The first version was released in 2001 by Refractions Research under the GNU General Public License, and development has continued since then actively. In 2006, PostGIS was certified as a compliant Simple Features for SQL database by the Open Geospatial Consortium.

There are a large number of software products that can use PostGIS as a database backend, including:

- Quantum GIS
- uDig
- GeoServer
- MapServer
- GRASS
- MezoGIS
- Feature Manipulation Engine
- Cadcorp SIS
- Ionic Red Spider
- OpenJUMP
- TerraLib
- TerraView

Quantum GIS

Quantum GIS is an open source GIS (mapping) application which is similar to commercial mapping packages. Because it is distributed as an opensource application under the GNU distribution license, Quantum GIS can be reprogrammed to perform different or more specialized tasks. There are also plug-ins available to expand compatibility and functionality. Quantum GIS has a small file size compared to commercial GIS's and requires less RAM and processing power; hence it can be used on older hardware or running simultaneously with other applications where CPU power may be limited.

It is a multi-platform application and runs on different operating systems including Mac OS X, Linux, UNIX, and Windows XP. Performance appears to be better on non-Windows machines. For Mac users, the advantage of Quantum GIS over GRASS GIS is that it does not require the X11 windowing system in order to run, and all around the interface is much cleaner and faster. Quantum GIS can also be used as graphical user interface to GRASS.

Quantum GIS is continually maintained by an active group of volunteer developers who regularly release updates and bug fixes. Currently, developers have converted Quantum GIS into 14 languages and the application is used internationally in the school and professional environment.

TerraView

TerraView is an GIS application built on the TerraLib GIS library. TerraView handles vector data (polygons, lines, points) and raster data (grids and images), both of them stored in a relational or geo-relational database, including ACCESS, PostgreSQL, MySQL and Oracle Spatial. TerraView has a visualization interface that allows attribute and spatial queries on object in geographical database. The interface allows different views on the database, producing thematic maps with different types of legends.

TerraView is able to manage raster data in geographical database and allows the visualization and manipulation of raster data together with vector data. Raster data can be shared in different formats such as GeoTIFF, TIFF, JPEG, RAW, ASCII-Grid or ASCIISpring.

TerraView supports vector operations including intersection and buffer maps. It also has statistical analysis functions: local and global autocorrelation indexes, semivariograms, and regionalisation.

Notable commercial or proprietary GIS software

Most widely used notable proprietary software applications and providers:

Autodesk

Autodesk, Inc. (NASDAQ: ADSK), a Fortune 1000 company, is a software and services company for the manufacturing, infrastructure, building, media and entertainment, and wireless data services fields. Autodesk was founded by John Walker and twelve other co-founders in 1982. Over its history, it has had various locations in Marin County, California, USA. It is currently headquartered in San Rafael, California.

Organization

Autodesk is divided into four industry-specific business divisions: *Manufacturing Solutions* (MSD), the *Architecture, Engineering*

& Construction (AEC), the *Media and Entertainment Division* (M&E), and *Platform Solutions & Emerging Business* (PSEB), which includes geospatial and plant solutions, content and search, and extended design as well as Autodesk Labs. Autodesk also has a services group, Autodesk Consulting, and the *Location Based Services Division* (LBS).

Portfolio

The *Platform Solutions and Emerging Business* division develops and manages Autodesk 's flagship product, AutoCAD, AutoCAD LT, Autodesk 's Geospatial solutions, Plant solutions, Extended Design offerings such as Design Review, Content and Search solutions, Autodesk Labs, and worldwide engineering.

The *Manufacturing Solutions Division* develops and manages Autodesk Inventor Series, Autodesk Inventor Professional, AutoCAD Mechanical and Autodesk Vault.

The *Architecture Engineering and Construction* division develops and manages Autodesk AutoCAD Architectural (Old name - Architectural Desktop), Autodesk Building Systems, Autodesk Revit Architectural (Old name - Revit Building), Autodesk Revit Structure, Autodesk Revit MEP (Old name - Revit Systems), and Autodesk Civil3D.

The principal product offerings from the Media and Entertainment Division are Maya, 3ds max, *Discreet Inferno, Discreet Flame, Discreet Fire, Discreet Flint, Discreet Smoke, Toxik* and *Lustre.* These Academy Award winning products are covered on a dedicated page for the Media and Entertainment Division. Other products include Autosketch, Autodesk Subscription Program and Autodesk LocationLogic.

Discontinued Products

From time to time Autodesk discontinues some of the products in their portfolio. Some of Autodesk's "retired" products are listed here:

- Volo View was a web-enabled review and markup tool from Autodesk for engineering data, including support for Autodesk's DWG, DXF, and DWF formats. Volo View enabled design teams to communicate ideas and review designs without access to AutoCAD software. Autodesk discontinued sales of Volo View on May 1, 2005. The latest version of the software, Volo View 3, worked with the following file formats: AutoCAD 2004, DWG and DXF; Design Web Format (DWF 6); Autodesk Inventor 7 IPT, IAM, and IDW and raster files. The functionality of this product is largely replaced by Autodesk Design Review. Autodesk has also released a free product called DWG TrueView. This product enables users to view and plot AutoCAD DWG and DXF files, and to publish these same files to the DWF file format.

- Autodesk Animator Pro (DOS) and Autodesk Animator Studio (Windows) were products designed for cell based animation produced between the early to mid 1990s. At the time Autodesk was also advertising a Autodesk Media product similar in description to Macromedia's Director but this product was never released to the public.
- Cyberspace by Autodesk was an early real time 3d environment capable of producing basic phong shaded walkthroughs of DXF format models in "realtime". No textures were supported, and the system appeared to support a maximum DXF model size of around 35kb. A popular demo model of the Parthenon in Greece was shown around the US in a tour of the portable demo system - complete with virtual reality goggles. on the September 30th, 2004 Autodesk announced that QuickCAD would be discontinued after version 8.

History

Autodesk 's first notable product was AutoCAD, a CAD application designed to run on the systems known as "microcomputers" at the time, including those running the 8-bit CP/M operating system and two of the new 16-bit systems, the Victor 9000 and the IBM Personal Computer (PC). This CAD tool allowed users to create detailed technical drawings, and was affordable to many smaller design, engineering, and architecture companies.

Release 2.1 of AutoCAD, released in 1986, included AutoLisp, a built-in Lisp interpreter initially based on XLISP. This opened the door for third party developers to extend AutoCAD's functionality, to address a wide range of vertical markets - strengthening AutoCAD's market penetration.

Subsequent to AutoCAD Release 12, the company stopped supporting the Unix environment and the Apple Macintosh platform. After AutoCAD Release 14, first shipped in 1997, Autodesk discontinued development under MS-DOS, and focused exclusively on Microsoft Windows.

AutoCAD has grown to become the most widely used CAD program for 2D non-specialized applications. The native file formats written by AutoCAD, DXF and DWG, are also widely used for CAD data interoperability.

In the early 1990s, Autodesk started to develop specialty versions of AutoCAD, targeted to broad industry segments, including architecture, civil engineering, and manufacturing. Since the late 1990s, the company has added a number of significant non-AutoCAD-based products, including Revit, a parametric building modeling application (acquired in 2002, from Massachusetts-based Revit Technologies for $133 million), and Inventor, an internally developed parametric mechanical design CAD application.

On January 10, 2006, Autodesk acquired Alias, with its automitive styling and digital content creation applications, for $197 million USD. On August 6, 2007, Autodesk announced the acquisition of Skymatter Inc, developer of Mudbox.

On August 28, 2007, Autodesk announced the acquisition of California-based PlassoTech, developers of CAE applications. Terms of the transaction were not disclosed.

Autodesk 's products compete against products from several companies, including MicroStation from Bentley Systems, VectorWorks from Nemetschek, ArchiCAD from Graphisoft, SolidWorks, owned by Dassault Systemes, Solid Edge from Siemens UGS PLM Software, 12d Model, owned by 12d Solutions, Pro/E from PTC, and SDS/2 owned by Design Data.

ESRI

ESRI was founded as Environmental Systems Research Institute in 1969 as a privately held consulting firm that specialized in land use analysis projects. The worldwide headquarters of ESRI are anchored in a multicampus environment in Redlands, California.

ESRI 's business involves the development and support of GIS software, with customers including small businesses, large corporations, non-government organizations (NGOs) and governments at all levels.

ESRI has offices throughout the United States; a business partner program with more than 2,000 developers, consultants, resellers, and data providers; and a network of more than 80 international distributors with more than a million users in more than 200 countries. ESRI hosts an annual International User's Conference, which has been held in San Diego for the past 10 years. An estimated 14,500 worldwide users attended in 2007.

Products

ESRI uses the name ArcGIS to refer to its suite of GIS software products, which operate on desktop, server, and mobile platforms. ArcGIS also includes developer products and web services.

Desktop GIS

ESRI 's current desktop GIS suite is version 9.2, which shipped in final release form in November, 2006. ArcGIS Desktop software products allow you to author, analyze, map, manage, share, and publish geographic information. ArcGIS Desktop comes in three levels of licensing: ArcView, ArcEditor and ArcInfo. ArcView provides a robust set of GIS capabilities suitable for many GIS applications. ArcEditor, at added cost, expands the desktop capabilities to allow more extensive data editing and manipulation, including server geodatabase editing. ArcInfo is at the high end and provides full, advanced analysis and data management capabilities, including geostatistical and topological analysis tools. At all levels of licensing, ArcMap, ArcCatalog and ArcToolbox are the names of the applications comprising the desktop package.

ArcReader, ArcExplorer, and ArcGIS Explorer are basic freeware applications for viewing GIS data.

ArcGIS Desktop Extensions are available, including Spatial Analyst which allows raster analysis, and 3D Analyst which allows terrain mapping and analysis. Other more specialized extensions are available from ESRI and third parties for specific GIS needs.

ESRI 's original product was ARC/INFO, a command line GIS product available initially on minicomputers, then on UNIX workstations. In 1992, a GUI GIS, ArcView GIS, was introduced. Over time, both of those products were offered in Windows versions and ArcView was offered as a Macintosh product. The names ArcView and ArcInfo are now used to name different levels of licensing in ArcGIS Desktop, and less often refer to these original software products. The Windows version of ArcGIS is now the only ArcGIS Desktop platform that is undergoing new development for future product releases.

Server GIS

Server GIS products allow GIS functionality and data to be deployed from a central environment. ArcIMS (Internet Mapping Server) provides browser based access to GIS. ArcSDE (Spatial Database Engine) is used as an RDBMS connector for other ESRI software to store and retrieve GIS data within a commercially available RDBMS. Currently ArcSDE can be used with Oracle, DB2, Informix and Microsoft SQL Server databases. It supports its native SDE binary data format, Oracle Spatial, and ST_geometry. ArcGIS Server is an internet application service, used to extend the functionality of ArcGIS Desktop software to a browser based environment. ArcGIS Server is available on Solaris and Linux as well as Windows and will eventually phase out ArcIMS. Other server based products include GIS Portal Toolkit, ArcGIS Image Server and Tracking Server as well as several others.

Mobile GIS

Mobile GIS conflates GIS, GPS, Location-based services, handheld computing, and the growing availability of geographic data. ArcGIS technology can be deployed on a range of mobile systems from lightweight devices to PDAs, laptops, and Tablet PCs. Products: ArcPad, Mobile ArcGIS Desktop Systems, ArcGIS Server (Server-oriented APIs), ArcWeb Services (Web-oriented APIs) and hosted geographic databases.

Developer GIS

Developer GIS products enable building custom desktop or server GIS applications or embed GIS functionality in existing applications. These focused solutions can then be easily deployed throughout an organization. Products: ESRI Developer Network or EDN, ArcEngine (Desktop-oriented APIs), ArcGIS Server (Server-oriented APIs and a web development ADF which is part of ArcGIS Server), ArcWeb Services (Web-oriented)

Hosted GIS (ArcWeb Services)

ArcWeb Services give a diverse user community access to geospatial content and capabilities. Central to ArcWeb Services is the geographic data it aggregates, and a variety of geographic services such as map display and address geocoding. ArcWeb Public Services are free to developers building non-commercial, non-governmental applications. ArcWeb Commercial Services provides fee-based access to additional capability. Products: ArcWeb Services—Commercial Services , ArcWeb Services—Public Services, and Web-oriented APIs.

Microsoft MapPoint

Microsoft MapPoint is both a technology ("MapPoint Web Service," previously known as MapPoint .NET) and a specific software program created by Microsoft that allows users to view, edit and integrate maps. The software and technology are designed to facilitate the geographical visualization and analyzating of either included data or custom data. Numerous acquisitions (Vexcel, Vicinity, GeoTango, etc.) have supplemented both data and feature integration.

MapPoint is intended for business users but competes in the low-end GIS market. It includes all of the functionality of the most recent version of Streets and Trips at the time of development, as well integrates with Microsoft Office, data mapping from various sources including Microsoft Excel, and a Visual Basic for Applications (VBA) interface allowing automation of the MapPoint environment.

The MapPoint technology is used in

- **End-user software:**
  - MapPoint (for North American and Western European business users)

- AutoRoute (for Western European for home and small business users)
- Microsoft Streets and Trips (for North American typical home users)
- Encarta encyclopedia

❑ **Web-based services:**
- The MapPoint web service
- The Microsoft Maps website mappoint.msn.com
- The MSN-based Virtual Earth virtual globe service.

Microsoft MapPoint as the software is typically updated yearly and available in both upgrade and full packaged product form, the current version being 2006, which significantly updated GPS integration and features. Previous versions were released starting with 2000 (developing from Expedia Streets, a consumer mapping application included with Office 97 Small Business Edition), which was slated to be included in the Office 2000 Premium Edition suite, but never

Subsequent releases followed in 2001 (very similar to 2000, and more of a data update), 2002, and 2004. New versions have not always been at the same time as the equivalent Office releases despite being numbered similarly; notably the 2002 release was excluded from the Office XP suites due to a lack of equivalent programmability, and 2006 was released well before Office 2007. The program's icon and toolbars have also not been updated since the 2002 release to stay consistent with the current Office suites.

Other notable proprietary software applications and providers:

CARIS

CARIS Ltd. is a company which produces Geographic Information System (GIS) and hydrographic data processing software.

Universal Systems Ltd. (USL) was founded in 1979 as a spin-off from GIS research conducted at the University of New Brunswick and was initially focused on marketing CARIS GIS (an abbreviation for Computer Aided Resource Information System) in terrestrial applications. The company was renamed to CARIS from USL several years ago in recognition of its first product and most-recognized brand. It is based in Fredericton, New Brunswick, Canada.

CARIS operates in direct competition with companies such as ESRI and Intergraph. USL also cooperated with the Canadian Hydrographic Service in pioneering the development of 'ping-to-chart' applications for the hydrographic industry. Other important markets include GIS for the cadastral and geological industries, and a range of other applications are also produced including a web map server. CARIS is a member of the Open Geospatial Consortium and is a proponent of interoperability between different GIS systems.

GMS (software)

GMS (Groundwater Modeling System) is a complete program for building and simulating groundwater models. It features 2D and 3D geostatistics, stratigraphic modeling and a unique conceptual model approach. Currently supported models include MODFLOW, MODPATH, MT3D, RT3D, FEMWATER, SEEP2D, and UTEXAS (in version 6.5 beta).

Version 6 introduced the use of XMDF (eXtensible Model Data Format), which is a compatible extension of HDF5. The purpose of this is to allow internal storage and management of data in a single HDF file, rather than using many flat files.

History

GMS was initially developed by the *Engineering Computer Graphics Laboratory* at Brigham Young University (later renamed in September, 1998 to *Environmental Modeling Research Laboratory* or EMRL) in the late 1980s on Unix workstations. It was developed primarily for The United States Army Corps of Engineers and is still known as the *Department of Defense Groundwater Modeling System* or *DoD GMS*. It was later ported to Microsoft Windows platforms in the mid 1990s. Version 3.1 was the last supported version for HP-UX, IRIX, DEC-OSF, and Solaris platforms.

In April 2007, the main software development team at EMRL entered private enterprise as Aquaveo, LLC, and continue to develop GMS and other software products, such as WMS (Watershed Modeling System) and SMS (Surface-water Modeling System).

Oracle Spatial

Oracle Spatial forms a separately-licensed option component of the Oracle Database. Oracle Spatial aids users in managing geographic and location-data in a native type within an Oracle database, potentially supporting a wide range of applications from automated mapping/facilities-management and geographic information systems (GIS), to wireless location services and location-enabled e-business.

Componentry

Oracle Spatial provides a SQL schema (named by default "MDSYS", where "MD" stands for "Multi Dimensional") and functions that facilitate the storage, retrieval, update, and query of collections of spatial features in an Oracle database. Oracle Spatial consists of:

- A schema that prescribes the storage, syntax, and semantics of supported geometric data types.
- A spatial indexing system.
- Operators, functions, and procedures for performing area-of-interest queries, spatial join queries, and other spatial analysis operations.
- Functions and procedures for utility and tuning operations.
- A topology data model for working with data about nodes, edges, and faces in a topology.
- A network data model for representing capabilities or objects (modeled as nodes and links) in a network.
- A GeoRaster feature to store, index, query, analyze, and deliver GeoRaster data (raster image and gridded data and its associated metadata).

The spatial component of a spatial feature consists of the geometric representation of its shape in some coordinate space referred to as its "geometry".

Availability

As of Oracle version 10.2, potential users can elect to license Oracle Spatial with Oracle Enterprise Edition. Oracle Personal Edition bundles Oracle Spatial for no extra charge.

Oracle Spatial does not run with Oracle Standard Edition, with Oracle Standard Edition One or with Oracle Express Edition (XE) although a version of Spatial, with reduced functionality, named Locator is provided with these editions.

History

The Oracle RDBMS first incorporated spatial-data capability with a modification to Oracle 4 made by scientists working with the Canadian Hydrographic Service (CHS). A joint development team of CHS and Oracle personnel subsequently redesigned the Oracle kernel, resulting in the "Spatial Data Option" or "SDO" for Oracle 7. (The SDO_ prefix continues in use within Oracle Spatial implementations.) The spatial indexing system for SDO involved an adaptation of Riemannian hypercube data-structures, invoking a helical spiral through 3-dimensional space, which allows n-size of features. This also permitted a highly efficient compression of the resulting data, suitable for the petabyte-size data repositories that CHS and other major corporate users required, and also improving search and retrieval times. The "helical hyperspatial code", or HHCode, as developed by CHS and implemented by Oracle Spatial, comprises a form of space filling curve.

Since Oracle 8, Oracle Corporation marketing has dubbed the spatial extension simply "Oracle Spatial". The primary spatial indexing system no longer uses the HHCode, but a standard r-tree index.

4

Digital Mapping Technologies in GIS

Introduction

Digital mapping technologies include computer-assisted mapping tools such as GIS, satellite image-processing software, and Global Positioning System (GPS) field collection devices.

Comparison of Traditional Cartography and Digital Mapping Techniques

Cartography is the "art, science and technology of making maps, together with their study as scientific documents and works of art". A comparison of digital cartography with traditional cartography reveals the benefits available through computer mapping. A case will be made that digital cartography is faster, more efficient, and more powerful and versatile than analog cartography. This comparison will be discussed regarding data sources, process, and products.

DATA SOURCES

Traditional, manual, or analog cartography is typically dependent upon data sources such as previously published maps, aerial photography, or some form of annotated geographic data, such as field notes or surveyed sample points. These data sources are expensive as well as voluminous, so they tend to be stored in specific isolated locations. The isolation of the data reduces access by data users to what is perceived by the owner of the data as a fixed asset.

Digital cartography utilizes the same types of data sources as analog cartography but has access to a wider pool of digital data sources from previously performed digital projects. Traditional cartography is constrained to the use of a published map or set of maps and often requires redrafting of information from the old maps to the new map. In contrast, digital cartography makes immediate use of existing digital data to update or create a published map.

Another component of the wider data pool is a growing set of products which were designed for use in a digital format and which are distributed via the Internet or CD-ROM. Internet users are able to identify new sources of information and retrieve data almost instantaneously. The CD-ROM hardware is inexpensive and provides easier access to larger digital data files (600 megabytes) than was practical with the floppy disk drives associated with personal computers (1 megabyte) or with the tape drives associated with mainframe computers (50 to 100 megabytes). One example of the type of data that is being widely distributed by CD-ROM is the 1:1,000,000 scale *Digital Chart of the World*.

The entire set of satellite imagery also must be considered in the growing library of digital data, particularly with the advent of the Earth Observing System (EOS) planned under the National Aeronautics and Space Administration's (NASA) Mission to Planet Earth (Lillesand and Kiefer 1994). EOS sensor systems are being designed to provide a wide array of data sources for global and, in particular, tropical assessments.

Developers of digital databases are still susceptible to the institutional forces which tend to support division and isolation and to the political forces which tend to reduce access to data. However, it is the experience of the author that digital cartographers are aware of their reliance on widely disseminated data sources and tend to add their data to the wider pool.

PROCESS

Analog cartography produces a map as its final product. The map is a static object which provides a snapshot of some set of spatial phenomena at a set time. Digital geographic analysis offers the ability to process data in a variety of ways. The process of analysis is interactive and is usually iterative built layer by layer. Digital analysis of geographic data allows several maps to be treated concurrently, thus building an understanding of relationships between the various mapped phenomena. This capacity has led to the development of numerous geographic models.

A geographic model represents spatial and temporal aspects of reality in digital terms. For example, a model that estimates soil loss may use rainfall, land cover, soil, and slope data to identify areas with the highest erosion potential. The ability to represent complex processes in a way that is easy to interpret has created a high demand for GIS technologies by decision-makers and policy analysts.

Digital processing also is conducive to combining geographic data from a variety of scales. For example, it is difficult to interpret simultaneously information from a soil map at a scale of 1:200,000 and an elevation map at 1:50,000 scale using traditional cartographic map sheets. However, GIS allows the user to generate slope and aspect maps from the elevation data and to change the scale of the new data to 1:200,000 for direct overlay with the soil data. Thus, trends can be identified using digital analysis that would not be obvious through visual interpretation of the two map sources.

One noteworthy feature of the storage structure of digital data is that some information is carried inherently in the system. For example, area totals for the various classes in a GIS map do not need to be estimated using laborious techniques as in traditional cartography since they can be reported instantaneously on the computer. The storage of data in a format conducive to statistical analysis is the foundation for the entire discipline of image analysis as it has developed. Quantitative techniques in geography have revolutionized both the research time frame and the types of questions that can be posed.

Digital cartography often stops at the same point as traditional cartography, providing a similar product whose only difference is in the form of generation or the medium of delivery. However, GIS differs from computer mapping of a static map in that GIS generates new information through geographic analysis.

PRODUCTS

Digital mapping technologies and analog cartography also can be compared in terms of the quality of their products. One of the most cost-effective benefits associated with digital cartographic products is that they can be updated efficiently. For example, incorporation of changes in traditional cartography typically requires redrafting, but digital cartography requires that only the changed features be updated.

Many digital products were designed to define baseline conditions in order to detect and monitor future change. For example, a land cover map indicating forested vegetation in 1975 can be superimposed on a 1995 land cover map to measure forest loss and to identify the locations of greatest loss.

Automation is the process of computerizing. The operation of automating geographic analysis is itself a product independent of the set of maps produced, particularly in technology transfer. Automation requires a standardization of procedures and a degree of centralization of data. When a resource agency is able to bring its data to a standard of quality sufficient to release to other agencies, then that agency benefits from having more usable data. Likewise, the evolution of data exchange mechanisms between agencies has direct benefit to all agencies and to the management of the public resource. Conservation and resource management is increasingly interdisciplinary and interdepartmental in nature. Building the capacity to contribute to and receive from the rapidly growing body of data is a valuable product.

Implementation of Digital Mapping Technologies in Tropical Developing Countries

It is useful to evaluate the costs and constraints in implementing digital mapping technologies. Successful applications have been demonstrated in the utilization of image analysis, GIS and GPS. The three technologies have been applied in measurement of deforestation, identification of suitable habitat for various species, and a variety of protected area wildlife management issues.

However, the initial investment in advanced mapping technologies is high, and many remote sensing technology transfers have failed to address the unique conditions of the recipient country. The reasons for failure in technology transfer within developed countries are similar to the causes of failure of technology transfer in tropical developing countries, but the quality of conditions in tropical developing countries makes technology implementation more difficult.

The implementation of an information technology such as GIS or image analysis can be evaluated along the three major components of the information system hardware and software, data, and staff. The concept of the GIS as a triangle was developed by the author to stress the balance required in investments and activities in each of the three components in a well-functioning information system. A successful implementation plan should address all three components. Excessive focus often is placed upon hardware and software considerations, particularly if competing vendors are involved. Often, agencies are eager to acquire the hardware and software, and vendors are eager to close the sale. If the other two system components are not realistically evaluated at this stage, it is possible that an agency will be left with a powerful computer processing capability and insufficient funds to hire skilled staff or to run projects.

Figure 4.1. Three major components of an information system. Implementation of an information system should be balanced along each component. The presence of any two components should produce the third component.

The third component will naturally evolve in a system where two of the components are well-managed and appropriately funded.

For example, an agency can make an investment in hardware and software and then make a parallel investment in trained staff. Staff who are given a designated time period to provide a return on the investment of the initial purchase and to cover a specified percentage of their salaries should be able to leverage their available hardware and their free time to start profitable projects.

There are alternative combinations of the presence of only two positive components in the system triangle. Talented staff who have a project or are handling data which would benefit from the acquisition of hardware and software will either purchase additional resources through the project or utilize existing capabilities under entry-level conditions. Successful project performance will provide justification for advances in hardware and software in future activities.

Also, consider the presence of sufficient equipment and a project that needs to be performed. An agency will be forced to allocate staff for the project if it is to be completed. The level of importance of the project will determine the level of staff commitment. It is impossible to achieve successful project implementation without appropriate staff commitment. If full-time staff cannot be assigned to the project, then at least 50 percent of a staff person's time should be designated for handling all of the issues associated with data manipulation and system maintenance. Part-time staff cannot devote sufficient attention to the complexities of managing an information system or to the data requirements of a successful project. An agency that cannot assign someone at least half-time to the system should contract the work to an outside party in order to accomplish the objectives of the project.

When systems only exhibit one strong component, then it is unlikely that they will succeed. An example of this condition resides in an administrative unit which invests in the hardware and software or receives a grant that provides the same. Insufficient allocation of trained staff to use the system will result in poor quality of data or inferior project performance. Typically, a project that includes a set of application objectives in addition to system implementation does not allocate sufficient time for the system implementation. It is unrealistic to expect even a trained staff to garner funds for the start-up costs of hardware and software as well as salary costs. If it were necessary to invest initially in only one of the three system components, then an investment in the best available staff would have the most probable success.

The balance of this section will address current trends and developments in each of the system components and particular conditions of the three components in relation to tropical developing countries.

Hardware and Software

Hardware costs for both personal computers and workstations have been declining steadily during recent years. This trend, combined with the rapid increases in computer processing speed, has dramatically benefited the GIS market. Geographic data are voluminous and require several unique hardware and software adaptations for data entry, processing, and output. These adaptations are referred to as hardware peripherals and include digitizers, scanners, and plotters. With a healthy GIS market, these peripherals have become more sophisticated, easier to use, and less expensive. The GIS market also has supplied a variety of hardware and software configurations from which to choose. Although increased choices provide more opportunities for the end user, the choices are often overwhelming for those entering the digital mapping arena.

Three guidelines facilitate the decision processes associated with selecting hardware and software. First, a low-cost information system, such as one based upon a personal computer (PC), has low risk in terms of investment and high returns in staff training. Software such as IDRISI is PC-based and has a short learning curve which enables the generation of faster output from a project. Networked and stand-alone workstations have more sophisticated requirements for implementation than PCs. Software such as ARC/INFO which operates on the more advanced hardware systems tends to have a steep and long learning curve. A successful PC implementation may develop into needing more advanced hardware, but the growth should be balanced along the three system components.

The second guideline in the selection of hardware and software is to evaluate the quality of support. If a hardware or software company is a leader in its field, then its technical support infrastructure is likely to be more accessible and informative than that of a small company. This consideration is particularly significant if the unit is geographically remote. Hardware support and maintenance are critical. One dysfunctional element in the system can severely impair the entire system. If assurance cannot be obtained that hardware will be serviced or replaced rapidly, then an alternative hardware selection should be considered.

Third, a wide variety of peripheral hardware devices should be considered with full awareness of the temporal limitations of all the devices. Whichever data entry, storage, display, or output device is selected, it is likely to become outdated technology or insufficient for growing needs in a short period of time. It is advisable for management staff to accept this fact at the outset and solicit the recommendations of staff rather than limiting the ability of the technical staff to keep the system current. One benefit of this phenomenon in information systems is that a unit can start out small, knowing that it will be upgrading almost continuously. Another benefit is that outgrown technology can be maintained as backup equipment or it can be used by entry-level personnel or students.

DATA

GIS databases are increasing in availability. The United States has benefited from the government publication of 1990 census data which have been distributed along with 1:100,000 scale road and stream data for the continental United States. The provision of a consistent national digital framework has allowed GIS users to have a readily available base map upon which to build. Numerous digital geographic databases have been published in recent years and are available over the Internet. The availability of high-quality satellite data also has facilitated numerous environmental mapping applications. Satellite imagery is a particularly rich data source because the availability of historic data from the 1970s enables the creation of a consistent baseline from which to perform change detection.

Although there are more data available in the public domain or at a nominal cost, satellite data prices have increased over the last twenty years. Further, the need to add specific information layers to existing data sources adds to the data costs of a given project in salary time for data entry. Also, field efforts are typically required in conjunction with digital mapping applications. Walklet suggests that data costs can account for as much as 80 percent of total information system costs over the life of the system.

Collection of traditional and digital data in the tropics has been constrained by the number of scientists working there, the economic realities associated with the fact that many tropical countries are developing countries and thus less equipped to fund database construction, and the physical difficulty of collecting data for remote areas. The first two constraints are beyond the arena of digital mapping technologies, but the third constraint has been addressed by the utilization of satellite data in mapping remote areas.

Satellite image processing or remote sensing has provided the capability to map some areas of the world that were difficult and more expensive to chart using traditional techniques. Unfortunately, there is not as much satellite imagery available for the tropical regions of the world as is available for the temperate zones because there is more cloud cover present in the tropics. In most cases, cloud-free images can be pieced together, but the process requires use of multiple images often temporally distinct by as much as two to three years. Even if the cost of data acquisition can be reduced through data grants or data-sharing mechanisms, the processing time remains high because of the need to handle more images. In many final image analysis products, areas under cloud cover remain unmapped, and reliance is placed upon combining aerial photographic data sources or other previously mapped data with the output from the image analysis to map these areas.

The use of radar imagery has long held promise for use in the tropics since it can be collected day or night and has the ability to penetrate cloud cover. However, radar data are less readily available than other satellite data sources. Further, radar has unique processing requirements for which many image analysts are not trained. The advent of radar sensors in the planned EOS platforms should alleviate the data availability and cost constraints, but the international community must allocate resources to training in radar data processing.

STAFF

The high demand for professionals trained in GIS and image analysis has been constant as the digital mapping industries have grown. The supply of skilled analysts is more acute in the tropical developing countries. The phenomenon of "brain drain," where individuals who gain advanced training pursue opportunities outside their home countries, often limits the ability of a country to increase its technical capacity. In a GIS workshop held in San Jose, Costa Rica, for natural resource managers, the most commonly listed weakness in current GIS operations were staff shortages and inadequacies in training programs.

The issue of staff may be better understood in the tropics as an issue of training because it is likely that a resource professional already on staff will be given additional digital mapping responsibilities. In this case it is important to realize that in order for the individual to perform digital mapping functions well, several conditions should be met. The percentage of time allocated for digital mapping functions should be clearly specified if it is necessary for it to be less than 100 percent. The tasks associated with mapping technologies are so varied that it is difficult for an individual to be productive if he or she also is assigned a variety of unrelated functions.

The digital mapping staff should not be perceived as the hardware experts for the agency simply because they are proficient in hardware concerns. The digital mapping staff should have expertise in hardware, software, and the specific set of applications (forestry, soils, etc.). It is rare that one individual is skilled in all three areas. The software expertise may reside with a hardware expert or with an applications expert or be shared by both. It is difficult for an applications professional to remain current in a suite of hardware concerns, and it is unrealistic to expect a hardware professional to be skilled in an applications area. If possible, two people should fill complementary roles.

Ample support should be provided to the staff. The support may be in the form of additional compensation, discretionary budget to acquire the resources they deem necessary to perform their job, or in permission to travel to attend conferences or training courses. The frustration level of digital mapping staff can be high, and any effort directed to making their job easier will increase the chance of retaining valuable staff. The significance of the role of the staff component in computer systems should not be underestimated, particularly in computer mapping where the demand for trained professionals exceeds the supply.

One approach to maximizing investment in training the applications staff in digital mapping technologies is to select a familiar development path and build around that technology. For example, staff who are already performing aerial photo interpretation may be able to gain the necessary skills in image analysis in a time period shorter than the two semesters which would normally be required. Likewise, staff who are already collecting field data will be able to be trained in the use of GPS receivers more effectively than office staff. GPS training can be obtained in less than a week. An agency that develops either image analysis or GPS capability can then invest in building GIS capacity. Also, it is possible for an agency to contribute to collaborative project efforts between agencies and allow other parties to address the more complex issues associated with GIS. The collaborative approach allows staff in the agency developing GIS capacity to gain exposure to issues of database design, data integration and analysis, and cartographic output. Development of staff abilities through partnerships with other agencies will enable those staff to make recommendations on GIS development based upon their direct experience.

If agencies are able to accept their constraints and to identify where areas of interagency cooperation could help all parties to maximize limited resources, then there is a possibility that data sharing and collaborative training programs will enable those agencies to balance their investments along all three components of information systems.

5

Image Analysis in GIS

Basic Concepts

Remotely sensed data include a variety of data sources that are defined from the range of the spectrum of electromagnetic radiation. Aerial photography is used to capture reflective signals from the visible and near-infrared portion of the spectrum. Most digital scanners operate in similar portions of the spectrum. Thermal and radar sensor systems are sensitive to a different portion of the energy spectrum.

Remotely sensed data provide an operational GIS with timely and synoptic data. Image analysis techniques are commonly utilized to perform regional vegetation mapping and to update existing vegetation maps. The utility of a sensor system for the detection of surface phenomena must be assessed along four dimensions: spatial resolution (area or size of feature that can be identified), spectral resolution (number and width of electromagnetic bands for which data are collected), radiometric resolution (detector sensitivity to various levels of incoming energy), and temporal resolution (frequency of satellite overpass). The four satellite sensors that are addressed in this chapter are (in decreasing order of spatial resolution) Advanced Very High Resolution Radiometer (AVHRR), Landsat Multispectral Scanner (MSS), Landsat Thematic Mapper (TM), and Satellite pour l'Observation de la Terre (SPOT).

Airborne and satellite digital sensors collect and store data values for discrete units of the surface of the earth. A scene is composed of a large matrix of these cells. Each cell is referred to as a picture element, or pixel, and may correspond to a square meter, hectare, or square kilometer, depending on the sensor. The spatial resolution of the sensor is usually expressed as the length of one side of the cell. AVHRR has a spatial resolution of 1.1 kilometer; MSS resolution is 79 meters; TM is 30 meters; and multispectral SPOT is 20 meters.

The spectral resolution of a sensor refers to its ability to capture data in a certain portion or band of the electromagnetic spectrum. The spectral resolution of AVHRR is five bands; MSS has four bands; SPOT has three bands; and TM has seven bands. Sensor bandwidth refers to the range of energy units recorded by a sensor. Most sensor systems have several sensors on board, which results in concurrent data collection across multiple bands. For example, all Landsat sensors have had a green and a red band and at least two infrared bands. The Landsat TM sensors have a blue band and infrared bands additional to the MSS sensors. Visible energy has wavelengths of 0.4 to 0.7 micrometers, near-infrared energy has wavelengths of 0.7 to 1.3 micrometers, mid-infrared energy has wavelengths of 1.3 to 3.0 micrometers, and thermal infrared energy has wavelengths of 3 to 14 micrometers.

False color composite prints that are similar to color infrared photographs can be generated from these satellite data, but the true power of the digital data lies in the ability to statistically assess each band of the spectrum independently or in combination with any or all of the other bands. For example, a body of water and a patch of forest may both have high brightness values in the green band, but the forest emits infrared energy in contrast to the water, which absorbs infrared energy. Thus, water and forest are readily discriminated using only one band of data. It may be necessary to use several bands of data to classify different types of forest, in which case probabilities are assigned to each pixel as to its membership within a given cluster of spectrally similar pixels. Digital image analysis is a process that was built around the statistical techniques of such information extraction. Land use and land cover maps are one type of map generated from the image analysis process.

The radiometric resolution of the MSS sensor is lower than the other three sensors. The MSS sensor records brightness values between 0 and 63 for a given pixel in each of its bands. The other sensors are sensitive to a range of 0 to 255. Thus very subtle differences in the spectral properties of a material may not be discriminated as well using MSS data. For example, if the brightness values associated with a material were exactly 50 percent of the maximum reflectance in all bands, then MSS would record 32 and TM would record 127 for each band. A difference in a TM band for two materials might result in brightness values of 126 and 129, but the MSS sensor could only record a value of 32 for both materials.

The temporal resolution of the sensor refers to the frequency with which imagery is obtained for the same geographic area. AVHRR provides daily coverage of the earth, whereas TM collects at most twenty-three images of an area per year. MSS temporal resolution is eighteen days for Landsat 3 data and sixteen days for Landsat 4 and 5 data. The temporal resolution of SPOT data is variable, eleven to twenty-six days, depending on whether sidelook data are desired. The SPOT satellite has the capability of collecting side-look imagery at an angle of up to 27 degrees, thus improving the probability of collecting cloud-free data.

The two major classification techniques in image analysis are unsupervised and supervised. The unsupervised classification approach statistically assigns each pixel to a cluster or class based upon the probability distance of the pixel to similar clusters when considering all the various bands of data. The unsupervised approach requires the user to label the classes according to the best understanding of the spatial distribution of all the members of a given class after the processing is complete. A supervised approach is different from the unsupervised technique in that it requires "training" data upon which to initiate the statistical classification program. The algorithms assign each pixel in the remainder of the image to a class based upon the statistics associated with the training data. Both approaches require ground truth data from other maps, aerial photography, or from field observation. In the supervised approach the ground truth data are used first, and in the unsupervised approach they are used last.

Although the use of remotely sensed data is becoming common, it is an expensive technique because of the cost of satellite imagery acquisition and processing. Staff specialists and image interpretation software and hardware are required. As a result, few areas within Central America have existing satellite classification maps. AVHRR analysis of all of Mexico has been completed, Landsat scenes have been analyzed in the Yucatan, and NASA airborne sensors have been utilized in Belize. Extensive analysis has been performed in Costa Rica.

Review of Habitat-Mapping Capability of Four Sensors

The four sensors have been assessed for the purpose of mapping habitat as an input to gap analysis. AVHRR has utility in monitoring greenness, but has limited utility in mapping vegetation types because of its coarse spatial resolution. SPOT has several advantages over other sensors, but it is limited by its spectral resolution, notably missing the mid-infrared band. Sensors with bandwidths recording mid-infrared energy are useful in vegetation analysis because of the water absorption characteristics of leaves, which are spectrally detectable.

The tendency to misclassify areas because of too fine a spatial resolution is another weakness of SPOT (also present in TM but to a lesser degree). For example, patches of trees within a pasture can be classified accurately as isolated pixels of the forest land cover. However, the land use of the area is pasture, so the ability to convert land cover data to land use data must be considered in the image analysis process.

TM is the sensor of choice for gap analysis, primarily because of its high spectral resolution and its adequate spatial resolution. MSS is a second choice to TM, primarily because of its reduced spectral resolution. MSS has only four bands with the two infrared bands in the near-infrared rather than the mid-infrared.

The conclusions of Scott are valid, but cost considerations require an evaluation of MSS and AVHRR in addition to TM. International conservation mapping should utilize satellite data that cost the least and are able to be integrated meaningfully with wildlife and protected area data sets. It is useful to distinguish between three levels of vegetation mapping and the satellite systems that can support each level: AVHRR for global surveys with scale ranging around 1:2,000,000 and with discrimination between forest and nonforest; MSS for national surveys with scale ranging from 1:250,000 to 1:1,000,000; and TM or SPOT for local surveys with scale ranging from 1:50,000 to 1:100,000.

Successes and limitations of the various sensors utilized in tropical forestry applications have been reviewed. It was found that AVHRR has its highest value as a tool for identifying the geographic areas most suitable for more detailed imagery analysis. Various biophysical parameters such as net primary productivity have been generated for global studies using AVHRR, but they are least accurate in the complex ecosystems of the tropics. MSS has proven successful in numerous cases of change detection, particularly in the identification of areas of deforestation. However, MSS studies have had mixed results in identifying secondary growth other than young secondary growth and in discriminating forest species consistently. Published results of TM analyses are relatively few, and very little has been published on SPOT investigations in the tropics. TM has been utilized successfully in the identification of relatively undisturbed primary forest. However, old secondary forest and disturbed primary forest were indistinguishable, and confusion occurred between secondary forest and regions of mixed crops. The four sensors clearly vary in their utility in habitat mapping applications.

AVHRR

AVHRR applications have been reviewed by Hastings and Emery. Most of the examples of terrestrial surface mapping address general trends associated with vegetation indices or thermal aspects of the sensor such as snow cover mapping or forest fire monitoring. In terms of change detection, AVHRR has been shown to have utility in detecting forest clearing in Amazonia. Early work done in Africa with AVHRR by Townshend and Justice and by Justice, Holben and Gwynne indicated that vegetation indices had potential in vegetation monitoring, particularly if a strong seasonal component can be measured.

More recent efforts in North America indicate the utility of AVHRR in producing regional vegetation maps. A multitemporal analysis made use of various ancillary databases to produce a land cover characteristics database for the conterminous United States. A similar project was performed for Mexico. The level of detail associated with Mexico's classes of natural vegetation are temperate forest, tropical dry forest, tropical high and medium forest, and scrub vegetation.

A combination of the thermal data of AVHRR with the visible data may prove useful in discriminating finer levels of vegetation information than has been achieved previously using AVHRR. Because of the strong commitment to global change programs and the growing attempts to more fully exploit AVHRR data as a regional mapping tool, it is likely that further advances in its application will be achieved in the near future. The level of vegetation mapping done for North America and Mexico using AVHRR is currently being extended to Central America.

MSS

MSS data have been utilized in assessing deforestation trends in Costa Rica. The study targeted identification of primary forest, disturbed forest, and cleared lands, but relied on several ancillary data sources to accomplish its objectives. These data sources included digitized versions of previously prepared forest inventories, life zone maps, and elevation data.

MSS was utilized also in a deforestation study in Guinea, West Africa. This study was similar in approach to the Costa Rican MSS analysis in that a variety of additional data sources were utilized in conjunction with MSS. The Guinea study produced more detailed information about patterns of shifting agriculture and degradation by erosion because it utilized aerial photography and videography.

In both studies MSS was found to be useful, but only because it was able to be utilized with other previously existing data sources or more powerful sensor data. The level of vegetation mapping that was expected from the MSS data was also relatively low. In an ongoing attempt to monitor regional trends of global change, MSS is being used as a historical baseline data source. The Landsat Pathfinder project is comparing historical MSS data to recent TM data, but the resulting change detection classes are constrained to the level which MSS can consistently produce: forest, deforestation, regrowing forest, water, grasslands, and clouds/cloud shadows.

TM

The increased information content associated with TM imagery was demonstrated in a project in which six forest and five nonforest classes were mapped in Minnesota. The level of analysis that can be achieved using TM data is supported further by the work of Moran.

The classes produced in their vegetation maps included not only forest, pasture, crop, bare, wetland, and water but also various stages of secondary growth: initial, intermediate, and advanced. A two-pass image analysis was performed that combined unsupervised and supervised classification techniques.

Evans, Schoelerman and Melvin also report advances in level of information extraction utilizing similar logic in the design of a TM analysis in Louisiana. A supervised classification was made of the TM image producing a six-class map of open/harvest areas, pine regeneration, pine, hardwoods, mixed, and water. A second pass was made over the pine class to break out low- and high-crown density subclasses. Congalton, Green, and Teply describe an elaborate methodology to map the distribution of old growth forests in the Pacific Northwest using TM imagery. Both supervised and unsupervised classification methods were employed. Extensive field data were available, and ancillary data were often used to differentiate vegetation classes that were spectrally indistinguishable but were located at distinct positions of elevation. Remote sensing was utilized to identify crown closure, size class, and structure to build species-level identification.

Each of these projects utilized detailed data for training statistics and applied a second or third level of analysis to achieve higher information content. Such effort is necessary to link local change detection analyses with regional and global mapping efforts. A similar theme is evidenced at an institutional level in the call by Justice to increase partnerships between international agencies and local experts. The question of scale is applicable both in bridging global and national inventories and in creating more collaboration between international and national scientists and resource managers.

SPOT

Very little has been published on the efficacy of SPOT data in habitat mapping, particularly in the tropics. A five-class habitat map was successfully produced using SPOT data in India. Rasch describes a project in the Philippines that produced twenty-two habitat classes, comparable to the level achieved with TM (previously described). The unique benefit of SPOT in the Philippines project was the ability to produce cloud-free imagery in a shorter time span than could have been generated through TM data acquisition because SPOT has a market-driven schedule for data acquisition. Pohl describes an Indonesian mapping project that merged SPOT with ERS radar. The combined strength of the SPOT sensor in spectral and spatial resolution with the cloud penetrating capability of radar resulted in the production of a 1:100,000 scale image useful for updating existing maps.

The trade-off between the increased spatial resolution offered by SPOT and the lower spectral content has not been fully evaluated, in particular regarding forestry applications. A comparison of SPOT and TM in detection of gypsy moth defoliation in Michigan indicated that the performance of SPOT was 4 to 8 percent worse than TM in generating maps of defoliation and nondefoliation.

Most of the identified literature on SPOT is similar to Ehlers and Johnson emphasis is on the advanced spatial resolution and the associated ability of performing more effective urban mapping. Additional information on SPOT applications in the tropics could probably be obtained in the French remote-sensing literature. Further, because of the commercial interests of many of the SPOT users, fewer results might get published in the technical literature. A recent SPOT newsletter indicated that SPOT data are being utilized extensively in Brazil and Bolivia, but the level of success of projects on the mapping of tropical habitats in these countries has not been assessed.

Utility of Satellite Imagery in National and Regional Conservation Mapping Efforts

Other variables must be considered in planning the image analysis component of conservation mapping efforts in addition to an assessment of the efficacy of a given sensor in habitat mapping. Data costs, data volume, data availability, and the probability of alternative sensor solutions all have advantages and disadvantages which need to be evaluated independently for each country or region where habitat is mapped.

DATA COSTS

The most obvious factor in weighing the trade-offs between high spatial resolution sensors such as TM and SPOT and the lower spatial resolution sensors such as MSS and AVHRR data is cost. The higher spatial resolution data are much more expensive and cost $4,400 per TM scene and $2,600 per SPOT scene. Historical MSS scenes (older than two years) are available for $200, and AVHRR data costs $80 per scene. It also requires more SPOT scenes than Landsat and more Landsat scenes than AVHRR to cover the same geographic region. Thus, coverage for Costa Rica using one AVHRR scene costs $80, while five MSS scenes cost $1,000, five TM scenes cost $22,000, and twenty-two SPOT scenes cost $57,200. There are numerous cooperative data acquisition programs in place which help to defray the costs of national or regional mapping programs. The existence of such cooperative agreements is variable geographically, depending upon the initiative of the natural resource agencies in a state or country to pool their investments in data.

DATA VOLUME

Differences in the spatial resolution of various sensors can translate to considerable differences in data volume, especially if compounded by a greater frequency of bands. For example, a geographic area measuring 240 meters on each of four sides would require a three-by-three array of MSS data, or nine pixels. Each pixel has four bands; thus the image would require 36 data values. The same geographic area covered by TM (which has 30-meter spatial resolution rather than the 80-meter resolution of MSS) would require an eight-by-eight array, or sixty four pixels. Six of the seven bands of TM data are typically used, thus there is a total of 384 data values. The TM data have over ten times the volume as the MSS, and this has repercussions in terms of the time required to process data as well as in the requirements for data storage.

The size of an AVHRR dataset is approximately 1 percent of the size of an MSS dataset for the same area. A country the size of Costa Rica (51,100 square kilometers) generates a habitat database with approximately 50,000 points if the 1-kilometer AVHRR sensor is employed. AVHRR may provide a good data volume alternative to both Landsat systems, particularly if the region being mapped is as large as the entirety of Central America.

There are advantages to using general sensor systems such as AVHRR. In assessing the utility of coarse resolution satellite data, Roller and Colwell list several benefits of synoptic sensors such as AVHRR. These benefits have immediate savings if certain compromises in spatial resolution can be accepted. The acquisition of a single database obtained at a single time eliminates the need to merge numerous adjacent images. It may be easier to acquire cloud-free or cloud-reduced imagery in certain areas with the higher temporal repetition (daily) available with coarse resolution sensors. It is possible that multi temporal analysis might compensate for some of the information loss associated with decreased spatial resolution.

DATA AVAILABILITY

Most imagery of the tropics has limited data availability due to extensive cloud cover. For many areas, a computer search of all available imagery may result in only one or two dates of imagery having less than 20 percent cloud cover. One can acquire multiple dates and use the cloud-free areas in both images, but this is expensive and may not solve the problem. Further, there are possible temporal complications which could affect classification results. For example, it may be difficult to discriminate between different vegetation classes unless imagery is collected during an optimal season of the year. Analysis of imagery from two distinct seasons of the year may result in different classification results.

If cloud cover is a severely limiting constraint, it may be necessary to employ a multiple-sensor approach. The additional platform could be any of the higher cost systems to ensure better data for those areas. The other data sources may include aerial photography or airborne videography, depending upon the information needed and the budget of the project. Videography and other sensors are covered in the following section.

There are plans to complete regional AVHRR mapping of Central America. However, it is not yet certain that national composite maps of Costa Rica and the southernmost countries can be generated using AVHRR, due to the high cloud cover at the time of day of satellite overpass. The extent of the cloud cover may limit the utility of the map or database for the entire country of Costa Rica, but the data for the majority of the Central American region may remain viable.

Alternative Sensor Solutions

The focus of this chapter has been on four satellite platforms. Although these systems have been the most commonly used in habitat mapping, there are numerous other systems becoming operational or being planned for the near future. The most significant for tropical applications is radar imaging. Radar has had appeal for tropical habitat mapping for some time because it has the ability to provide data in spite of cloud cover. However, airborne radar data have been expensive and difficult for many image analysts to interpret. With the advent of space borne radar systems on recent Canadian, European, and Japanese satellites, and on the planned American EOS and the Russian Almaz-2, a more consistent data source is anticipated than the early short-lived satellite radar systems. An evaluation of the utility of current space borne radar systems for mapping in the tropics found that the multiple radar bands in the EOS configuration holds the greatest potential for vegetation mapping in the tropics.

It is possible that the Moderate-Resolution Imaging Spectrometer (MODIS) sensor planned as part of the EOS program may provide a database that is neither as general as AVHRR nor as voluminous as Landsat. MODIS will collect data at three spatial resolutions 250, 500, and 1,000 meters and will collect thirty-six bands of data, including spectral data similar to the TM sensor.

Airborne videography also is a cost-effective data collection technique, particularly if used in conjunction with other sensor systems. A multi sensor approach on board a single aircraft was used to map vegetation in the Arizona gap analysis project. Continuous video was captured in conjunction with regular acquisitions of photography taken at two different scales, in order to compare samples of the video with higher resolution data. The airplane also was collecting positional data with a GPS receiver; thus all the airborne imagery could be combined with other geo-referenced data such as Landsat TM.

Forthcoming Databases

There are several efforts to construct regional databases. Justice documents two major international tropical mapping programs. The first is the forest assessment being done by the United Nations Food and Agricultural Organization (UNFAO). UNFAO forest assessments conducted for 1980 and 1990 utilized Landsat and AVHRR data for select regions of the world with a goal of continuous coverage. The NASA Landsat Land Cover Change Pathfinder Tropical Deforestation Project is analyzing three image dates between the mid-1970s and 1989 for approximately one thousand MSS scenes in large tropical regions such as Amazonia, Southeast Asia, and Central Africa. The geographic and temporal status of these programs and the quality of their results should be evaluated in relation to specific project needs when designing any national or regional conservation mapping programs.

The disadvantage of waiting for any database is that it may be delayed or canceled. Further, the data quality for a particular region may be lower than that required by the user. There are serious cost advantages to waiting, not only in data acquisition but also in staff time allocated to processing the data. One might identify avenues of collaboration and cooperation in ongoing projects that are helpful to both the local and the international mapping efforts by investigating the prospects of waiting or advancing independently.

6

GIS Design and Implementation

Introduction

Biological research stations are growing in number and becoming more sophisticated in the services they provide. It is not uncommon for researchers to have access to full meal services, air-conditioned laboratories, libraries, and computers. More comfortable living combined with access to research equipment allows researchers the opportunity to stay longer at the site, thereby becoming part of an atmosphere that promotes the integration of data, information, and knowledge. One of the mechanisms available for this integration is access to computer-based tools such as GIS and Database Management Systems (DBMS).

Techniques associated with GIS and DBMS are not new to research and government agencies. Their popularity also extends into various disciplines including geography, ecology and biology. In these fields GIS allows for the combination of diverse, geographically referenced data in a computer environment for storage, query, and analysis. Additionally, GIS provides users with a structured environment in which data from various sources can be integrated and analyzed. For example, it becomes possible to examine impacts of socioeconomic development on biological conservation. Before the availability of such tools, combining data from multiple sources was difficult and often not attempted. Tools such as a GIS/DBMS in the data collection environment makes this possible.

This case study shows how the installation of a GIS/DBMS at one field station La Selva Biological Station in Costa Rica is bringing tools for multidisciplinary research directly into the research environment. The important aspects addressed are the differing needs of the station administrators and the researchers, the integration of station-managed databases with researcher data sets, and the techniques used to provide data, computer access, and training. These concepts will be described by discussing the design study, the actual implementation, and the impact the system has had on administration and research at the station.

La Selva Biological Station

The Organization for Tropical Studies (OTS), founded in 1963, is an international consortium of about fifty universities, colleges, museums, and research institutions with the common goals of education, research, and conservation in the tropics. OTS promotes and supports a wide variety of basic and applied research at three field stations in Costa Rica. The largest of these is La Selva Biological Station, located in northeastern Costa Rica.

As a result of improvements in roads, public transportation, and dedicated OTS staff, La Selva has grown from a small isolated field station to an easily accessible research facility. This growth can be seen by the increase in the number of researchers that have visited the station: from fifty-seven researchers in 1982 to 240 in 1992. In 1992 alone La Selva hosted more than one hundred undergraduate and graduate courses as well as a variety of conferences and workshops in such diverse fields as agroforestry, biology, botany, ecology, herpetology, mammalogy, and ornithology. In addition to growth in research and education, the physical plant has been expanded to include a library, air-conditioned laboratories, conference rooms, and housing for up to seventy people per night. Even the actual size of the station has grown to include approximately 1,500 hectares of lowland tropical rain forest. The property consists of primary and secondary forest, abandoned pastures and plantations, managed habitats, and a 45-kilometer trail system.

The administrative activities at La Selva are also expanding at an increasing rate. In 1985, as part of La Selva Master Plan, OTS implemented a database policy. This policy requires researchers to submit key data for archive when requested by the station administrators. Before this policy researchers would collect data and return to their home institutions, thus restricting the data access of other researchers.

The station's growth, coupled with the need to examine data historically and across disciplines, demanded a new environment to manage station and researcher data; simply archiving was not enough. This need forced station administrators to investigate new computer tools, including GIS and DBMS, as a means to support the increased growth.

The Design Study

Before an integrated GIS/DBMS system can be successfully implemented, a design study should take place to identify the needs of all potential users. Systems implemented without designs often fail, not from technological limitations but because the system has not met the needs of the users. Design studies are either undertaken from within the organization or outside consultants are hired. In the case of La Selva, the study was conducted through a graduate-level geography course offered at Ohio State University.

Ohio State Design Study

Following the design approach recommended by Dr. Duane Marble, twenty Ohio State University graduate students divided into groups and formed questions for La Selva administrators and researchers. The researchers were selected based on their potential interest in GIS applications as indicated by the station's codirectors, Drs. Deborah A. Clark and David B. Clark. Questions focused on the database design and expected outcome:

1. What data do you expect to be included (e.g., soils, topography)? what scale?
2. What data would you provide? what is the original format of the data?
3. Do you have any previous GIS experience?
4. What products/analyses do you expect?

In brief, the goal of La Selva GIS is to be a tool shared by students, administrators, and researchers so that the combined use of the system generates cross disciplinary research and data integration. To meet this goal, the geographic database was fashioned in a hierarchical form, beginning with a detailed station survey and then expanding the database to the surrounding region. The hierarchical database allows for expansion so that researchers can contribute to the system at all geographic scales. Another result of the study was identifying the need for a full-time person to work at La Selva for user support. This would allow the system to support the on-site needs of the station administrators and the researchers. A final result focused on the physical components of La Selva 's infrastructure that are necessary to support a sophisticated computer system. To clarify these design results, a more thorough discussion of each follows. *Design Results* As a result of the design study, the following system goals were identified:

1. Build a geographically referenced database to facilitate new approaches to research at La Selva.
2. Assist the station administrators in making the decisions that directly affect the quality and type of research that takes place at the research station. For example, it is possible to use the GIS to analyze existing plot locations, trail locations, and forest cover to identify the locations of new research plots.
3. Design methods to help researchers use the database for project planning and spatial analysis.
4. Provide the flexibility to include regionally based projects so researchers can take advantage of the system's ability to manage large data sets.
5. Develop on-line demonstrations and training documents to help provide the means for everyone to use the facility.

It became apparent that La Selva system needed to include a nongeographic DBMS in addition to GIS. Tabular lists of flora and fauna, published and unpublished documents, and other information were in various forms at La Selva. To develop an integrated system effectively, these data needed to be included but were clearly not part of the geographic database. The DBMS portion of the database thus contains two types of data those collected by researchers to be made publicly available, and the data maintained by La Selva staff. Researchers provide digital data in a predetermined format with limited constraints to their accessibility as described in the database policy document. The core database maintained by OTS contains data representing general interests of the researchers and administrators such as researcher biographies, lists of flora and fauna, weather data, and herbarium records. The DBMS operates with the GIS so that relationships between the spatial distribution of certain features are associated with their nongeographic counterparts. For example, one of the geographic data layers is the distribution of researcher study plots. The user is able to link this geographic data layer with the lists of researchers involved in a particular study, resulting publications, key words, and collected data. The researcher data and the station-supported data all contribute to data archived at the station in both geographic and tabular forms.

Geographic database development started for La Selva region independent of OTS but, coincidentally, was concurrent with the design study. This database included topography, roads, hydrography, park boundaries, and political boundaries obtained from maps published by the Instituto Geografico Nacional (IGN). During the user interviews and with the aid of these data, it became apparent that a detailed survey of the research station was necessary. The interviews revealed that research scales vary from the entire station (approximately 1,500 hectares) to smaller than single hectare plots where individual plants are mapped. Even in the research projects involving the entire station, the maps published by IGN at 1:50,000 scale would not contain the detail necessary to identify spatial patterns for analysis. OTS decided to fund the development of a database with sufficient detail at the station level. Maintaining the plan for a hierarchical database, researchers have seen the database grow to be larger and more regionally defined, one that includes data from the adjacent national park as well as the initial data from the IGN maps.

In addition to the GIS-based data, remote sensing data are also incorporated into La Selva GIS and are being used by the researchers. These include images from airborne scanners, aerial photographs, and readings from radio telemetry. Uses of remote sensing in the tropics can include examination of forest/land-cover types to estimate deforestation rates and land use patterns, animal tracking through radio telemetry, and monitoring biodiversity.

During the design study, the computer resources in Costa Rica were found to be extremely limited, including technical support and personnel to run the machines. As a result, a system was designed to best support the users in a way that limited downtime would occur should problems arise with either the hardware, software, or databases. A second system running at the research station provides the first backup. A third system was donated by OTS to the Universidad Nacional (UNA) in the School of Geographic Sciences to help maintain and establish further links with the Costa Rican universities and to provide La Selva researchers with a system near San José.A fourth system plus technical support is provided through the Department of Geography at Ohio State University. This system is accessible to authorized La Selva users through Internet.

Providing multiple systems in several locations supports researchers while they are at the research station and when they are at their home institutions. The users of the GIS/DBMS are mostly biologists who are usually not trained in the use of GIS and may not wish to take the time to be trained in the technical aspects of GIS. In fact, many are not even aware of the hours required to design applications, enter data, perform analyses, and output the products typical to basic GIS projects. The users want quick results to sometimes fairly complex questions. To resolve some of these issues, the GIS at La Selva is designed to have these components:

1. a database manager to assist researchers with the design of projects that involve a GIS component;
2. menu-driven programs to aid in the development of geographically referenced databases;
3. programs to assist with the output of these data either in the form of maps or digitally transferable files; and
4. general recommendations on where to look for additional information about GIS and methods for analysis upon their return to home institutions.

These components, designed with the system objectives in mind, consist of databases and programs that are transportable to other systems, thus providing options and flexibility to the administrators and researchers. Details regarding these databases and programs will be discussed in the implementation section of this case study.

During the design study, a few potential problems were identified that would determine whether the computers required for the system would function at the research station. La Selva is a tropical research station where high temperatures and humidity are normal. Also, rural areas in Costa Rica do not always have consistent electric power. Power fluctuations and shortages that could damage the computers occur frequently. OTS addressed most of these problems long before the design study. The two laboratories, as well as the library, are air conditioned, and an electric generator capable of supplying power to the entire research station was in place for several years prior to the GIS/DBMS installation. In addition, surge protectors and uninterruptable power supplies were purchased for the GIS/DBMS. These are designed to help guard against electric surges and to maintain consistent power during the ten seconds it takes the generator to provide electricity.

Implementation

Critical to the development of an integrated database was the construction of a precise geographic database. As indicated by the design study, the publicly available maps would not contain the necessary detail for mapping and analysis.

OTS needed to construct a grid detailed enough to provide practical and accurate locations by researchers in the field. To meet these objectives, it was decided to construct a 50 × 100 meter topographic survey of the station. The accuracy of the grid is × 20 cm in the x, y direction and × 10 cm in the z direction. Also included in the survey were the trails, streams, station boundaries, building locations, and primary research plot boundaries. These data form the foundation from which the remainder of the geographic data are constructed.

To assist researchers in the field with the collection of geographically based data, a steel tube was placed at the intersection of each 50 × 100 meter grid line and labeled with a unique identification number. By using the fixed tubes, researchers can now map the location of trees, plants, animal sightings, study plots, and so forth based on the survey with a compass and a tape measure.

Although no protocols regarding quality control on data collection are established, the grid provides a better system for recording study locations. Previously, researchers would estimate their location based on approximate distances from unsurveyed positions on the trail. With the survey, data collected from the grid can be entered directly into the GIS and combined with the existing information in the hierarchical database.

To complement the hierarchical database design, remote sensing data were collected for the region. Sets of black-and-white aerial photographs from 1960, 1971, 1976, 1981, and 1983 were purchased from IGN. Each of these sets, at minimum, covers the research station property and most include significant portions of the surrounding area. The Canada Centre for Remote Sensing tested radar sensors in Costa Rica on two occasions and both included La Selva. Data from the first project, conducted in 1977, are not available. Data from the second radar project were collected in 1992 and are in place at La Selva. These include the radar data and a set of low-level color aerial photographs.

The National Aeronautics and Space Administration (NASA) also collected data from the area around La Selva. In 1988 NASA conducted a project to test two airborne multispectral scanners, as reported in Luvall et al. (1990). The two sensors, a Thermal Infrared Multispectral Scanner (TIMS) and a Calibrated Airborne Multispectral Scanner (CAMS), were tested over La Selva and most of the adjacent national park. Copies of aerial photographs taken as part of the project were donated by NASA. They include a natural color set and a false color infrared set for their entire study area. The TIMS and CAMS digital data are online at La Selva.

The non geographic data were more difficult to compile because existing tabular databases were in several unorganized formats. Some data existed only on paper; others were in various software packages; some were in many stages of completeness; and most were maintained by different people, on different computers, and in different countries. To compile these data it was decided to start simple and begin with databases that were already in digital form in Costa Rica. Concurrent with the construction of the tabular database in Costa Rica, a comprehensive structure was designed with the idea that new databases could be added without disrupting the initial design. An interface was structured to provide a direct connection between the GIS software and the DBMS software as the data were being compiled. Part of this link included the capability to transport the geographic and tabular data in ASCII format or in one of the export formats of the GIS or DBMS software in order to provide researchers a mechanism to take data home.

The GIS software being utilized is ARC/INFO because it provides a high level of programmer and user flexibility. Additionally, many of the OTS member institutions use it, thereby helping researchers apply what they have learned from La Selva to the systems at their home institutions. Sybase was purchased as the DBMS software because it is one of a small group of DBMS software packages with direct integration capabilities to ARC/INFO.

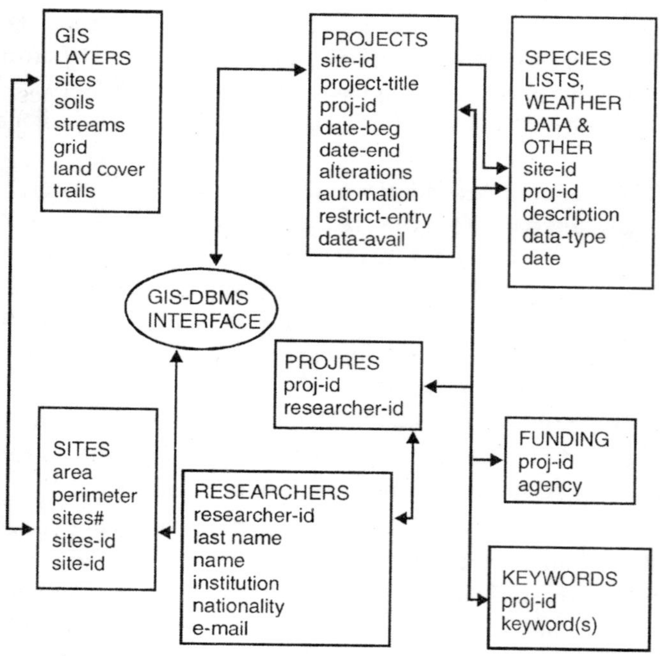

Figure 6.1. Design of the database structure for La Selva Biological Station.

The decision was made to use a DBMS software because they provide a Structured Query Language (SQL) interface not available through INFO alone. The hardware at the research facility includes two UNIX-based Sun workstations, two large digitizers, and two eight colour pen plotters. A local area network was installed, which includes three IBM compatible PCs and several Macintosh computers. These were established to facilitate data transfer and to allow for access to the databases from the administrative and public computers. The selections of hardware were made because the functionality of ARC/INFO increases at the workstation level and workstations have the ability to support multiple users.

Examples of Use

There are several potential applications that demonstrate how GIS is well suited to assist station administrators. The administrators need to maintain physical structures and monitor the research areas. The research use throughout La Selva can be monitored in GIS to avoid conflicts and maintain the quality of the forest. This type of site management is challenging because of the many variables to be considered: surface topography, trails, and existing research plots. GIS combines these variables, and the output is a composite of the variables that OTS can use to assist researchers locate new study plots based on their specific criteria and existing environmental conditions. For example, researchers may wish to locate a study area in a region that can be cleared; thus criteria might include presence of alluvial soils, little change in slope, and a specified distance from existing sites. GIS can combine these variables and display areas fitting these criteria. If researchers choose to locate their plot in this location, the new site boundaries and information about the researchers can then be added to the system.

Station administration was not the first project to utilize the GIS. A pilot project was established to polish the design and identify holes in the implementation. This project was a sixteen-month comparative ecological study of two of the primate species that coexist at La Selva: *Ateles geoffroyi* (red spider monkey) and *Cebus capucinus* (white-faced capuchin). A major component of the study included a comparison of the feeding patterns of these primates. Research included studies of feeding behavior as well as the spatial and temporal distribution of food resources used by the monkeys. While observing the monkeys, all trees that were used for feeding were marked with flagging. These trees were later mapped to the 50 ′ 100 meter grid. Before installation of the GIS at La Selva, each tree was plotted by hand on a paper map of the study site. After the installation, all mapped feeding trees used by both primate species were entered as point data into the project database. Associated attribute data (observation date, tree species, monkey species, etc.) were also entered to produce the feeding tree database.

Possibilities for GIS use in primate field research are vast and virtually untapped. Some of the topics being explored in this and future research serve to illustrate how GIS has expanded the possibilities for approaching challenging research questions such as understanding how the animals use forest space. The GIS calculated overall use area by comparing a variety of techniques. For example, area of use can be calculated by counting the number of 100 ' 100 meter grid squares that contain feeding trees, identifying a minimum convex polygon, or buffering the feeding trees. Examining how the use areas vary over time is critical in understanding how seasonal variation of food resources affects use of the forest. Area size is only one component to analyzing the spatial distribution of the species. Other factors to be considered are tree species density and diversity of habitat.

The specific results of these applications are unpublished and hence are not included in this document. The application of GIS to this study, however, has given the researchers insights into the spatial patterns of the food resources that could not have been obtained using previous methods (e.g., paper maps). As a result, future primate field studies by this investigator will likely expand on results obtained in the current study and include GIS in the initial project design.

Not all research projects at La Selva, however, are based on the movement of animals. Many studies are based on sedentary organisms (e.g., trees). Geographic analysis for these studies may examine tree growth spatially and temporally compared to slope, elevation, and soil type. Using the GIS and the 50 ' 100 meter grid, one project examined seven palm species found at La Selva. When comparing the mapped locations to soil type, topographic position, and accessibility for harvesting, four of the species displayed highly significant nonrandom distributions. It would have been difficult to obtain these results without the GIS.

The data collected and entered into the GIS from the primate project were among those used in the development of a poster and an on-line demonstration. The goals of the poster and demonstration were to introduce the concepts associated with GIS and DBMS and to begin to give potential users hands-on experience. Both were designed to illustrate the goals of the GIS at La Selva to appeal to students, administrators, and researchers and to aid in the evolution of their ideas for the GIS. Utilizing data collected from the primate project promotes data integration objectives to other researchers. In addition to the poster and demonstration, extensive training manuals were written to document the entry of data and the procedures for making maps and to provide samples of spatial analysis. For more information regarding GIS, users are encouraged to follow the training documents supplied with the ARC/INFO software. Although all projects at La Selva do not require explicit geographic analysis, these researchers benefit through the management of data sets, standard trail maps of the station, and the archive of databases.

When establishing a system like La Selva's GIS/DBMS, the primary goal is to create a solid foundation from which the system can continue to grow. This can only happen through adjusting the initial design and educating the researchers and administrators in the use of the tool. The design continues to be improved through interviews with users as they visit the station and interact with the training and demonstration materials. The user interviews identified and continue to emphasize the need for a common database for administrators and researchers. It is especially valuable to researchers because it is unlikely that individual researchers would construct a detailed system for personal use or integrate their data with other researchers. An advisory committee is being formed to formulate the future goals of the system. This group will be involved in setting priorities for the purchase of hardware and software, staff training, and database development and integration.

In general, the idea of data integration is supported by researchers but it is rarely practiced. It is also true that administrators have little control over data collection techniques and thus data quality. Various protocols can be written by station administrators, but they must be implemented and maintained. Despite these difficulties, the growth in research facilities demands better management of station resources, and a GIS/DBMS is one possible solution to these problems. This kind of facility should be maintained because it can be viewed as a centralized data archive for cross-disciplinary data and historical records of the research site.

The main objective for most researchers going to a research station is to collect data. Working at a computer in a laboratory can be viewed as inefficient use of resources during difficult financial times. A major problem with most GIS/DBMS is that the software programs are complex and training is expensive. As a result, many researchers are self-taught, and this requires a time commitment that may be impossible in some cases. As the technology becomes integrated into the research environment, researcher resistance to a new mode of working will diminish. Unfortunately, the technical staff available on the premises to train researchers and construct new databases is a further constraint. OTS operates on a limited budget primarily funded through grants and station fees. The problem is being addressed by providing users with portable databases, user-oriented programs, documentation, and systems based at home institutions.

Conclusions

There are many similarities between La Selva and other field-based research facilities. On-site facilities provide many benefits by addressing both researcher and administration needs creating a framework for multidisciplinary research and providing for easy and uniform archiving of data. These needs can be met through implementing a software and administrative system that institutionalizes data sharing and standardization by providing a framework for storage and analysis. Researchers can perform preliminary analysis on-site so that more or different data can be collected quickly. Data can also be verified and re-collected if errors are found. These benefits will be more apparent as the technology is incorporated into the normal operating procedures of the researchers at the station.

7

GIS Method for Conservation Techniques

Introduction

Gap analysis requires a map layer of the existing protected areas in order to assess the gaps in the conservation network. The boundary data on national parks and other protected areas in Costa Rica was provided by the Paseo Pantera project. The Paseo Pantera database includes protected area boundaries for the seven Central American countries south of Mexico. The data pertaining to Costa Rica were extracted from this database. The original source data were provided to Paseo Pantera staff by the National Parks Service of Costa Rica in the form of 1:200,000 map sheets indicating the boundaries of existing and proposed national parks, forest reserves, anthropological or tribal reserves, and private reserves. These data were digitized and stored in ARC/INFO format. Potential habitat linkage areas between parks were added by the Paseo Pantera staff but were utilized only nominally in this project.

A map of the protected areas is shown in figure 7.1 with the national parks indicated in black and the other protected areas indicated in gray. Although there is variation in the ability of national parks, forest reserves, and anthropological reserves to provide protection for wildlife, in this study there was no distinction made between different types of protected areas. For the purpose of the Costa Rica gap analysis, all protected areas were treated as equal. The proposed linkage data were not used in the initial application of the gap analysis in this project. Although the gap analysis methodology did not address variation in types of protected areas or in the proposed linkage polygons, an assessment of the distribution of wildlife sightings within the various types of protected areas and proposed linkages was made.

Habitat Conservation Decision Cube

The three decision vectors that form the Habitat Conservation Decision Cube are the three types of GIS layers utilized in gap analysis species distributions, habitat type, and protected areas. The wildlife, habitat, and protection map layers and the resultant possible combinations of these three geographic vectors can best be understood in the context of the Habitat Conservation Decision Cube presented and described in table 7.1.

Table 7.1. Eight Possible Policy Option in the Habitat Conservation Decision Cube Formed by the Presence and Absence of Wildlife, habitat, and Protected Area.

Decision Cube Option Areas	Wildlife (w)	Habitat (h)	Protected (p)
Wildlife protected	+	+	+
Conservation gap	+	+	–
Potential habitat restoration	+	–	+
Further wildlife study	+	–	–
Protected area data gap	–	+	+
Unprotected area data gap	–	+	–
Negotiation area	–	–	+
Developed area	–	–	–

Gap analysis has focused attention on one of eight possible combinations in the cube (wildlife present, habitat available, unprotected area) in order to identify optimal strategies for additional wildlife protection areas. The other seven possible combinations of the decision vectors also provide meaningful spatial information but are commonly left as unused by-products in gap analysis.

Hypothetical examples of the eight options in the context of the type of information each one supplies for conservation policy follow. The utility of this policy framework as applied in Costa Rica.

The *Wildlife protected* category (w+ h+ p+) exemplifies the ideal situation for wildlife conservation. From the point of view of wildlife conservation, these areas are the most effective and the highest priority areas in the park system. In terms of conservation management, it should be ensured that these areas continue to be managed according to the level of wildlife management standards currently employed. It might be useful for resource managers in the National Parks Service to assess further the *Wildlife protected* areas by comparing the percentage of that area in the national park system to the percentage of that area in forest and anthropological reserves. Such tabulation provides a mechanism for measuring how effective the park system is in meeting needs associated with wildlife management. It is possible either to highlight success in some areas for select species or to identify where additional management efforts could be allocated.

The *Conservation gap* category (w+ h+ p-) corresponds to the output from a typical gap analysis and identifies areas that should be added to the conservation system. For example, one review identifies several cases where gap analysis was used to recommend wildlife movement corridors for large mammalian species (Harris and Atkins 1991). The review examines potential habitat conservation areas of Florida panthers, grizzly bears in Yellowstone National Park, black bears in the eastern United States, and several African and Asian species. Although gap analysis serves as a tool to identify *Conservation gaps* potentially useful in corridor implementation, identified gaps must be assessed individually for their suitability to land acquisition strategies for the protection of wildlife. Variables that need to be evaluated include field verification of the number of species currently using the area, the population size of a species of concern, the relative status of each species (common, rare, endangered), and the suitability of the area for protection. A single map could be produced indicating areas most worthy of receiving additional protection or several maps might be produced for various species groups, i.e., birds, primates, and cats. These types of maps facilitate long term strategic planning for corridors between parks or for additional buffer areas around parks. The relative priority of identified gaps is not addressed at this phase of analysis. Additional information needs to be collected before making the economic and political decisions necessary to implement actions based upon the biological framework provided by the gap analysis.

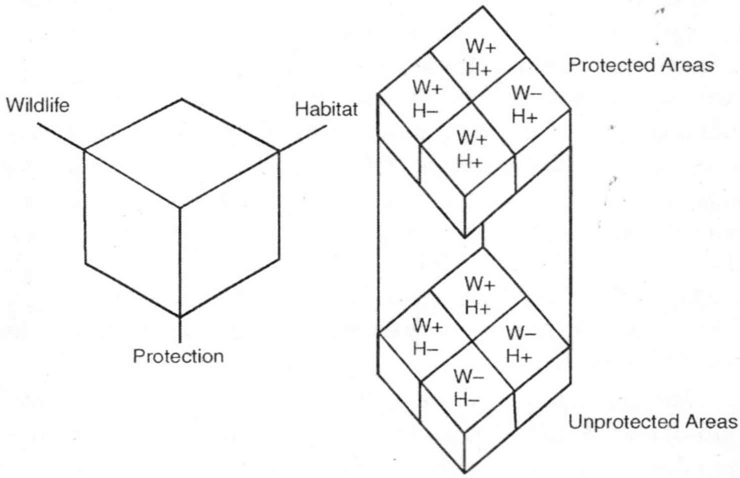

Figure 7.1. Habitat Conservation Decision Cube.

The *Potential habitat restoration* category (w+ h- p+) indicates areas where a species has been observed in a protected area in habitat not normally associated with that species. These geographic areas provide useful information in the selection of habitat restoration projects because they are already in some form of protected status. Management actions may be required to ensure future use of that portion of the protected area by a given species or group of species. Habitat restoration is typically an expensive conservation practice, but Jackson cites the work of Janzen in Costa Rica where tropical dry forest is being regenerated in conjunction with cattle grazing and fire prevention as a type of assisted natural regeneration. The gap analysis model is useful in identifying geographic areas that have potential for habitat restoration. However, field verification of a proposed restoration area is required to determine whether the area is logical or whether the identified polygon was associated with species edge behavior. For example, variable interpretation is required for data resulting from the sighting of a primate species, such as the white-faced capuchin, which utilizes a wider variety of habitat than a feline species, such as the margay, which is more selective in its habitat requirements. Thus, decisions about habitat restoration should be made in the context of an individual species or group of species as opposed to a general gap analysis performed on all species.

The *Further wildlife study* category (w+ h- p-) indicates areas which require further analysis by wildlife specialists in order to determine why a species was sighted outside its preferred habitat. The more detailed analysis should verify species presence in the unpredicted areas and assess edge behavior of the species. It may be necessary to relax the habitat requirements for a species. For example, if the number of sightings of a bird species is found to be equal in forested habitat and agricultural areas, then agricultural areas or at least a broad edge of agricultural areas should be included as the habitat for that species in future gap analyses. It may be found that the species is too much of a generalist to be used as an indicator species. Note that for both policy options where wildlife is present but habitat is not (*Potential habitat restoration* and *Further wildlife study*), it is possible that the species were sighted prior to changes in the habitat or that the species is utilizing small patches of habitat which cannot be resolved at the landscape level of analysis.

The *Protected area data gap* category (w- h+ p+) is one of two types of data gaps. Data gap polygons occur as a result of the presence of habitat data and the absence of wildlife data for a given polygon. It is not certain that the wildlife are absent from that area, only that wildlife data are not present. In a national survey, sightings cannot be expected in all suitable habitat areas, particularly where vast wilderness areas are concerned. *Protected area data gaps* also can represent areas where a species was extirpated prior to protection. For example, viable habitat for mountain lions still is present in the Great Smoky Mountains National Park, but the species is no longer present in the region. *Protected area data gaps* also may prove useful in the reintroduction of rare or endangered species, such as the red wolf program in the Great Smoky Mountains. A map of *Protected area data gaps* is useful in developing strategies for further field research on population distributions.

The *Unprotected area data gap* category (w- h+ p-) indicates areas that are similar to *Protected area data gaps*, both in terms of their data-uncertainty status in the gap analysis model and in terms of their biological potential. However, the unprotected areas do not warrant as great a need for further research as *Protected area data gaps* because the latter are more likely to be associated with some form of conservation action. An exception to this occurs when an *Unprotected area data gap* is adjacent to a protected area.

The *Negotiation area* category (w- h- p+) indicates areas that are neutral in terms of wildlife conservation and that hold potential as a point of negotiation for access to extractive industry within a protected area. For example, if the wildlife concerns are considered in the process of identifying a site for an agroforestry project, then these areas are much more attractive than sites having higher conservation status. It is possible that these areas may even be used to geographically trade for more desired corridor or buffers areas, either by altering management practices or by implementing legal changes in the park boundaries, thus generating enough revenues through sales to acquire more desirable lands. The *Negotiation area* category must be interpreted with caution. For example, an area identified in the center of a park is not as suitable as an area identified on the edge of a park. If *Negotiation areas* are utilized, it should be noted that maps only serve to define the negotiation process; numerous other forms of information will need to be considered before a trade is implemented. Trades or sales are advisable only to the extent that they do not compromise other goals of the park.

The *Developed area* category (w- h- p-) indicates areas that present another neutral case for wildlife conservation. Most of these areas are already developed or in agricultural use. Thus, these areas may be considered as the background in which wildlife conservation must operate. Mapping *Developed areas* in juxtaposition to protected areas is useful in the evaluation of proposed conservation areas because edge conditions of one proposed reserve may be superior to the edge conditions of another proposed reserve.

Interpretation of Results

Interpretation of the results in this project were performed at two different levels — the species level and combinations of species.

Gap analyses were performed individually for each of the twenty-one species, for all the species in combination, and for five species in combination. The first part of this section covers findings from all the gap analyses. The second part addresses wildlife frequency analyses which were performed. The third part of this section examines the policy options arising from the analysis of one of the species, the white faced capuchin. The fourth part of this section addresses the policy options arising from the analyses of five species and of all twenty-one species.

The two most important findings from reviewing all the gap analyses are as follows. First, there are few *Conservation gaps* identified for addition to the protected areas system in Costa Rica. The low incidence of *Conservation gaps* results from the percentage of the landscape already in the conservation system, and from the rapid deforestation of unprotected lands. This is reflected in the related facts of Costa Rica's strong commitment to conservation as expressed in its extensive park system, and in Costa Rica's 2.9 percent annual deforestation rate. In short, if land is not currently protected, then it is probably already cleared or will be in the near future. Trends in population growth and economic development will undoubtedly place new pressure on resource managers to maintain the integrity of the current conservation system. As a result, attention should be given to strengthening the quality of the existing system of protected areas. Evaluation of the utility of various protection categories (park, forest reserve, and anthropological reserve) in serving wildlife needs should facilitate continuous enhancement of wildlife management standards on all types of protected lands.

The second finding is the geographic extent of data gaps within the park system. There are some remote mountainous areas within protected areas in eastern Costa Rica which remain poorly described with regard to the wildlife data. A priority for further research in Costa Rica is to perform a more focused gap analysis on La Amistad International Park, which includes the major portion of the area under question. By combining the survey approach taken in this study with existing range data and with output from a predictive habitat model, it should be possible to develop a more robust wildlife data layer for use in the gap analysis model. It may be necessary to reduce the number of species of concern in order to achieve this objective.

Wildlife Frequency Analyses

The polygon overlay in the gap analyses that resulted in a series of maps, simple frequency tables were generated to assess the intersection of each set of species in the original wildlife point data with the protected area polygons. The national parks accounted for 718 (21 percent) of all the wildlife sightings. Fourteen percent of the sightings were on proposed linkages, 12 percent were on forest reserves, 5 percent were on anthropological reserves, and 1 percent were on private reserves. Almost half of the wildlife data points (47 percent) did not occur on any type of protected land or recommended linkage area. Concerning individual species, those species distributions that coincide most with the existing conservation network were the jaguar, mountain lion, tapir, and white-lipped peccary, with each having between 64 and 67 percent of its sightings in the protected area network. The point distributions of species which coincide the least with the conservation network were the squirrel monkey (15 percent coincidence) and the scarlet macaw (19 percent). The howler monkey, the white-faced capuchin, and the American crocodile had 28 to 31 percent coincidence. The remainder of the species ranged from 36 to 59 percent coincidence.

The results from the intersection of the wildlife points with the habitat polygons are presented in Table 7.3. Forty-seven percent of the wildlife sightings were coincident with some form of developed land use (pasture, agriculture, and urban). Forty-four percent of the sighting were coincident with natural land cover (forest, wetlands, mangroves, and subalpine scrub). Eight percent of the sightings were coincident with the unknown / mixed / clear category.

Single Species Gap Analysis

Each of the eight possible decision outcomes are reviewed using the example of the white-faced capuchin. The dark green polygons indicate *Wildlife protected* areas where white-faced capuchin are adequately protected. The red polygons indicate *Conservation gaps*. It is the relationship between these two categories that is significant in understanding the adequacy of the conservation system. The relationship between the *Wildlife protected* areas and the *Conservation gaps* needs to be interpreted visually and numerically. Visual inspection of the map allows interpretation of patterns such as

Table 7.2. Intersection of Wildlife Points with Protected Area Polygons.

Species	% Protected	Frequency of Sighting by Protection Status						Species Total
		P	F	A	L	PR	O	
Jaguar	65	39	15	5	5	2	28	94
Mountain loin	65	33	13	5	12	6	20	91
Tapir	64	53	24	6	13	0	33	129
Green macaw	64	16	16	1	5	1	19	88
White-lipped peccary	59	44	18	4	13	0	35	114
Harpy Eagle	48	8	11	0	8	0	13	40
Ocelot	48	23	22	14	20	5	50	134
Margay	42	32	14	10	16	5	68	145
Spider monkey	40	40	28	6	13	0	94	181
Central american caiman	38	29	22	12	16	0	85	164
White-faced capuchin	31	61	28	13	53	2	168	325
American crocodile	31	22	38	11	40	0	119	230
Howler monkey	28	44	23	6	39	0	151	263
Scarlet macaw	19	40	19	1	51	0	212	323
Squirrel monkey	15	13	4	1	10	0	50	118
Category Total	657	497	295	95	314	21	1,145	2,439

P = Parks, F = Forest Reserves, A = Anthropological Resources, L = Proposed Linkages, PR = Private, O = Outside Reserves relative proportion of one class to another and the proximity or isolation of the *Conservation gaps* in the context of the conservation system. Visual inspection also provides material for judgments about the general need for additional land acquisitions and the specific placement of those lands in a corridor pattern between protected areas or a buffer pattern around or adjacent to protected areas. There are twenty-three red polygons areas which serve as optimal land acquisition sites. Compare the fourteen isolated *Conservation gaps* to the nine *Conservation gaps* adjacent to protected wildlife areas. Given the limited resources that can be employed for the conservation of a given species, such visual assessment is useful in efficient allocation of those resources to strengthen the existing network. Conservation biologists and politicians in Costa Rica need to decide whether it is more effective to add new buffer zones to existing reserves or to strengthen genetic diversity by supporting the continued survival of an isolated ecosystem. Having a visual geographic platform from which to build a framework to evaluate such issues is the type of contribution that can be expected from a national or landscape-level gap analysis.

Table 7.3. Intersection of Wildlife Points with Habitat Polygons.

Habitat	Wildlife Sighting	Percentage
Natural land cover	1492	43.8
Forest	1238	36.4
Wetlands	133	3.9
Mangroves	111	3.3
Sub alpine scrub	5	0.1
Water	5	0.1
Developed land use	1642	48.2
Pasture	1382	40.5
Agriculture	228	6.7
Barren	28	0.8
Urban	4	0.1
Unknown/mixed/cleared	271	8.0
Total	3405	100.0

A numerical ratio indicates the relationship between *Wildlife protected* polygons and the polygons indicating *Conservation gaps.* The geographic area of both categories was tabulated, and it was determined that there are 2,150 square kilometers of *Wildlife protected* areas and 251 square kilometers of *Conservation gap* areas identified in the gap analysis for the white-faced capuchin. The ratio of *Wildlife protected* areas to *Conservation gap* areas is 8.6 to 1. If the ratio were reversed, then the species would be in serious need of conservation action because there would be considerably more area in *Conservation gaps* than in the *Wildlife protected* category. However, the case appears to indicate that the white faced capuchin has adequate conservation status in Costa Rica.

The same type of ratios were calculated for all twenty-one species. Species with the highest ratios include the tapir, mountain lion, and jaguar. These species are either adequately protected or they utilize only a nominal amount of land outside the protected area system. Species having the lowest ratios included the American crocodile, the great green macaw, and the giant anteater, but in each case the geographic area of *Wildlife protected* areas exceeded the geographic area of identified *Conservation gaps*.

Potential habitat restoration areas for the white-faced capuchin are indicated in light green in plate 4. These are non forested areas within parks which are being utilized by white-faced capuchins. In the case of Guanacaste, the large area indicated in northwest Costa Rica, much of the pasture is reverting to secondary growth forests on newly created park lands. An identification of similar types of areas strengthens the position of the resource manager in making recommendations for restoration. In the case of Tortuguero, the large restoration area indicated in northeastern Costa Rica, white-faced capuchins are utilizing forested wetlands. Although these areas are forested, a distinction was made between forest and wetlands in the habitat classification scheme, so these areas remain outside the defined habitat for white-faced capuchins. It is possible to relax habitat requirements and include wetlands with the forest as preferred habitat in future iterations of the model.

The relative proportion of pink areas in a species map was associated with the frequency of sightings outside forested habitat. Most species were similar to the white-faced capuchin in this category. Species having relatively few sightings, such as the harpy eagle and quetzal, occupied a small proportion of these areas. The tapir and three of the cats (the mountain lion, jaguar, and ocelot) also occupied a small proportion of these areas. The extent to which this is attributable to shy or nocturnal behavior or narrow habitat preference was not analyzed; however, some of the primate species appear to be more generalist in habitat requirements than the other species listed. It is probable that many of the areas for *Further wildlife study* were identified because the size of a patch of forest being utilized by the species was too small to map at the scale used in this study. For example, a squirrel monkey that was present in a very small patch of forest within a pasture would be interpreted as being present in the pasture and outside the forest habitat. It is also probable that many of the sightings occurred on the edge of a forested habitat and were inaccurately assessed as being outside the forest for reasons of geographic error.

Shades of blue were used to indicate geographic distributions of the four policy options for which there were no species present. The greatest concentration of *Protected area data gaps* is in La Amistad International Park. *Protected area data gap* polygons are present in many of the forested regions of Costa Rica, but the remoteness of the large tract of land in eastern Costa Rica indicates that there is a need to develop a broader understanding of wildlife populations in the country.

Many of the large *Unprotected area data gaps* are adjacent to the northern border of La Amistad. Also, these are steep forested slopes and are undeveloped even though unprotected. There are numerous small forest patches that fall into the *Unprotected area data gap* category because they meet the habitat requirement. These areas are of lower priority than the *Protected area data gaps* in terms of designating additional wildlife data collection efforts because of the manner in which the single large tract of *Protected area data gap* overwhelms all of the other data gap polygons.

Developed areas provide the background for conservation management. The Negotiation areas are of interest to wildlife resource managers because they indicate protected areas that may be negotiable from the wildlife perspective (though possibly not negotiable from the perspective of other park management objectives). If an area between two parks has been identified as a *Conservation gap* that is desired for land acquisition, it may be useful to know which areas within the park could be leased for sustainable extractive activities as part of an exchange for the desired land acquisition.

Multiple Species Gap Analysis

In many cases, it is advantageous to make conservation decisions on the basis of information supplied for an individual species. In other cases, it is informative to assess the distribution of the policy options in the Habitat Conservation Decision Cube for multiple species. This section addresses landscape patterns in Costa Rica when a group or all of the twenty-one species are considered concurrently. In each of the nine figures presented in this section, the boundaries of the protected areas are depicted for reference purposes.

The overlay of all the *Wildlife protected* areas for each of the twenty-one species indicates the extent to which the system of protected areas serves wildlife management purposes. The protected areas for which *Wildlife protected* polygons are absent either contain non forest habitat or are very remote or mountainous areas.

The total area of all of the *Conservation gaps* that were identified in the twenty one different gap analyses is displayed. Even when combining all the *Conservation gaps*, there are still not many tracts of land to evaluate at a more detailed scale. Most of the large *Conservation gaps* are adjacent to parks. Although a corridor pattern does not emerge, buffer areas are apparent. One noteworthy cluster for further evaluation occurs west of Tortuguero on the northern border of Costa Rica.

The areas in the *Potential habitat restoration* decision category are depicted. Much of the area in Guanacaste is undergoing restoration from pasture to secondary growth forest. The polygon near Tortuguero is a result of wildlife sightings in the forested wetlands habitat and is not an area requiring restoration. One of the small polygons near La Amistad is subalpine scrub.

Areas identified in any of the gap analyses requiring *Further wildlife study* are shown. These areas are primarily pasture and are associated with the large number of data points that were observed outside of forest. Because so much of the country is categorized as needing further study, this map indicates that not all maps are useful. The *Further wildlife study* decision category is most useful when applied to a specific species because a more manageable amount of information is generated.

When the two data gap categories were assessed in the multiple gap analysis, only those polygons without sightings were mapped. In contrast to the "or" logic used to create the maps where wildlife were present, maps of data gaps employed an "and" logic. For example, the data gaps for the harpy eagle are more extensive than the data gaps for the howler monkey because there were more howler monkey sightings. In the multiple species gap analysis, only the data gaps common to all species were mapped. The broad distribution of these areas throughout Costa Rica. Most of these areas are relatively small parcels of isolated forest. The large *Unprotected area data gaps* that are adjacent to protected areas should be considered equally with *Protected area data gaps* in the identification of further wildlife data collection efforts.

These areas need to be interpreted carefully and on an individual basis. If these areas have been compromised to some form of habitat degradation, then perhaps land use concessions may be employed to leverage acquisition of other lands. However, the areas may indicate unforested habitat that are protected (such as the large block of wetland areas near Tortuguero which are apparent in this map). The function that some of the areas within the park system may serve for species other than the wildlife that were examined requires evaluation. This study addressed only twenty-one of the hundreds of vertebrate species in Costa Rica. Likewise, these areas may be negotiable for wildlife conservation, but possibly not negotiable for other reasons for which parks are created.

An additional multiple species gap analysis was performed for five of the twenty-one species. This process was performed to compare gap analysis results obtained from the examination of twenty-one species to a multiple species gap analysis using a smaller set of potential indicator species. The species that were selected were determined by patterns of habitat utilization, geographic distribution throughout the country, and frequency of observations (compared to species utilizing similar habitat). The collared peccary was selected as one of the five species in order to represent those species that utilize undisturbed forest habitat as well as habitat in the more fragmented landscape. The white-faced capuchin was selected as the species to represent the four primate species that utilize undisturbed forest. The crocodile was selected to represent those species associated with rivers, forested lowlands, and wetlands. The jaguar was selected to represent the species that utilize extensive interior forests. The quetzal was selected to represent the species found in montane forests.

The five-species gap analysis was performed by combining all polygons that had the collared peccary, white-faced capuchin, crocodile, jaguar, or quetzal present, either alone or in combination. This set of polygons was intersected with the habitat and protected area map layers to identify *Conservation gaps*. The results of the five-species gap analysis were compared visually and numerically to the multiple species gap analysis that utilized all twenty-one species. The gray polygons indicate *Conservation gaps* identified by both of the multiple species gap analyses. The black polygons indicate *Conservation gaps* that were identified by the twenty-one species gap analysis, but were missed by the five-species analysis. Three of the five largest *Conservation gaps* were successfully identified by using only five species, but two of the largest *Conservation gaps* were missed. Of the two that were missed, one was used only by scarlet macaws and the other was used by margays, green macaws, great curassows, and giant anteaters. In general, the five-species gap analysis identified some, but not all, of the *Conservation gap* pattern in the landscape.

The numerical analysis measured the number of *Conservation gap* polygons that were identified by both multiple species gap analyses. The five-species gap analysis was successful in identifying 57 percent of the *Conservation gaps* identified in the twenty-one species gap analysis. The ability to use the five species to identify the *Conservation gaps* associated only with the other sixteen species was lower, with 39 percent of those *Conservation gap* polygons identified. If this set of indicator species were to be used instead of the larger set of wildlife data, the benefits in reduced data collection would need to be offset by the cost of reduced information content ranging from 40 to 50 percent. In some countries or regions, such a level of reduced information content may be acceptable. This would particularly be the case in countries where there are few protected areas and where information to develop conservation strategies is needed rapidly.

8

GIS for Identifying Priority Sites

Introduction

The Guanacaste area contains the main population of this animal in the country. The evaluation of the white-tailed deer's potential habitat in this area is very important since, in order to manage and conserve this valuable game-ranching species, it is necessary to know the quantity and quality of available habitat.

Different methods and techniques have been developed to analyze and evaluate the physiobiological variables of wildlife habitat in order to develop indices and models that will allow for the deduction of the appropriateness of a habitat for a specific species. For this purpose the following methods have been commonly used: biophysical habitat mapping; the regional evaluation of landscape for wildlife; multiple linear regression models; exponential regression models; habitat gradient models; wildlife and fisheries habitat relationships; and habitat evaluation procedures. The last method is the most widely used in evaluating wildlife habitat.

The habitat evaluation procedure, widely known as HEP, is a method developed by the U.S. Fish and Wildlife Service to measure the impact of changes carried out by land and water development projects. This method adapts to different management situations, including project planning, evaluations of environmental impacts, mitigation, compensation, and habitat management for fauna.

On the other hand, GIS actually represents a basic tool in gathering and analyzing data from the evaluation of land and aquatic habitats. Therefore, the use of this technology is fundamental to obtain a better combination and interpretation of the factors involved in habitat evaluation. The aim of this work is to construct a model to evaluate potential habitats for *Odocoileus virginianus* in the central district of Bagaces, Guanacaste, and to encourage future management strategies such as reintroduction, improvement of habitat quality, and the establishment of game ranching.

Study Area

The area of study is located in the medium and low basins of the Tempisque and Bebedero rivers. It comprises an area of 600.8 km^2 and belongs to the central district of Bagaces, Guanacaste. According to Bolaños and Watson's *Mapa de Zonas de Vida de Costa Rica* (Ecological map of life zones in Costa Rica), the following wildlife zones are identified for this area of study: tropical dry forest, wet premontane forest, and tropical wet forest. The average annual rainfall is 1,624 mm.

Materials and Methods

Location and Installment of Plots For the vegetation sampling, secondary and tertiary paths commonly used for horses were followed. These paths are well distributed throughout the area of study. Each path was mapped and subdivided into segments of 100 m length (for example one path with a length of 1,500 m, was divided into fifteen segments of 100 m each). To set the sample points, the sites were chosen at random from the N segments available in each path.

Once the sample point was located on the map, it was decided at random whether it would be on the right or left side of the path. In this manner a base map was created of the different sites where the sample points would be placed. In each of the sites identified as a sample point, five circular plots of 100 m^2 each were installed, twenty meters apart from each other. Five plots were installed in each sample point in order to obtain a better representation of the area and to maximize time and resources.

Some 0.01 percent of the total area was sampled. This percentage represents approximately 60.000 m^2,or six hundred circular plots of 100 m^2 each. To obtain the same sample intensity for the vegetation in all categories, the plots were distributed according to the percentage that represents the area of each category from the total area of study.

Recording of Field Information In each plot the following information was collected:

1. *Abundance of species.* All species of plants, bushes, and trees larger than 2 cm in diameter at breast height were recorded.

2. *Horizontal visual obstruction (vegetation cover).* The horizontal visual obstruction was measured with a piece of material 1.2 × 1.2 m divided into twenty-five black and white squares. Each square represented an area equivalent to 4 percent of the surface area of the material. The material was placed in the center of the plot at ground level, and the observer stood twenty meters from the material and recorded the number of visible squares. The number of visible squares was subtracted from the twenty-five total panels, and the percentage of covered area was calculated. Four measurements were obtained in each plot, with one reading from each cardinal point. Next, an average was obtained for each plot and for each category of current use and ground vegetation cover.

3. *Number of feces.* Only one count was made of fresh feces that were left by the deer on each of the established plots in order to obtain a preliminary validation of the model.

Creating a Database for the Area of Study

For a better analysis of the potential habitat of this species, a digital database of the zone of study was created using GIS, GPS, and remote sensors. The information sources that were used included the following maps:

1. *Map of current use and ground vegetation cover.* This map was based on the photo interpretation of aerial pictures with a scale of 1:35,000 (furnished by IGN), and it was complemented with a digital analysis of a Landsat satellite image (furnished by the TELESIG-UNA Laboratory). Next, the map was verified in the field.

2. *Map of springs.* In order to construct this map, each spring was visited and its position registered (latitude and longitude), with a 100 m margin of error using a GPS (Trimble Navigation 1992).

From the maps previously mentioned, the database included the following geospatial information provided by different institutions: map of land possession, map of communication lines, map of life zones, map of slopes, map of climate, map of permanent rivers, map of human settlements, map with the location of Stage II of the Arenal- Tempisque Irrigation Project, and map of capacity use for forest lands.

Later each map was digitized using the Roots program. The vector data were then exported to the IDRISI program. In IDRISI the files were stored in a 25 × 25 m format raster file. The commands used for the different analyses were area (area calculations), overlay (superimposition of maps), distance (measurement of distances), and crosstab (distribution of a variable in relation to a second variable).

Model For The White-tailed Deer's Potential Habitat

The scheme for the creation of the model was based on HEP methodology. This methodology assumes that the value of a wildlife area can be estimated using a habitat quality index with a scale of 0 to 1. The model structure consists of the following phases.

Assigning and Obtaining HSI (Habitat Suitability Index) Values The first step in the creation of the model was to assign HSI values (from 0 to 1) to each of the chosen variables and for each habitat present in the zone. Each habitat was assigned a value for the following variables: food, horizontal coverage, and slope of the terrain. This value (which varied between 0 and 1) represents the importance of the variable for the species. Next, by using GIS (IDRISI, command distance), HSI values were assigned to the other three variables (human activity, bodies of water, and distances between habitats) in the model since they are based on a distance analysis.

Once the HSI values were defined and assigned for each of the variables, six maps were designed that included the spatial distribution for each of the variables (with their corresponding HSI values). Then, using the sum function from the IDRISI-overlay command, the six maps were superimposed in the following manner. A map was obtained that included, for each site, six different HSI values (which represented six variables). Next, an HSI point average was calculated for the six variables to represent the final HSI for a specific site or point in the area of study. Mathematically, the formula to calculate the final HSI values is represented as:

$$HSI = (2v1 + 2v3 + 2v3 + v4 + v5 + v6) / 9$$

where the variables are: v1 = distance to bodies of water; v2 = food; v3 = vegetation cover for protection; v4 = slope; v5 = interdistances between habitats; v6 = human factors. Ecologically, this formula means that the variables for water, cover, and food will determine the habitat use of deer to a greater degree.

Finally, based on the distribution map for the different HSI values and on the limitation of the principal variables (water, food, and vegetation cover), the final map of quality of habitat potential was obtained for the species.

Relationships and Assumptions for Variables Used in the Model The present model was developed to evaluate the quality of habitat potential for the white tailed deer (*Odocoileus virginianus*) during the dry season. At the study area, the species is very vulnerable during this period owing to the decrease in vegetation cover caused by the loss of foliage and the frequent burning of pastures and woods. Furthermore, water is more scarce during the dry season, which favors the concentration of animals around water sources; this encourages illegal hunting.

Role of the Variables in the Model

Food. According to Gallina, the sites deer prefer are those that present higher plant diversity and biomass. For the present model, it is assumed that the more richness, abundance, and frequency of plants consumed by the deer in a determined area, the higher the value of that area for food resource.

Slopes. How slopes affect this species has not been evaluated in the zone nor in the rest of the country. However, X. Izurieta carried out a study in the zone of the Cotopaxi National Park in Ecuador and found that 96.8 percent of the deer (*Odocoileus virginianus*) sampled were found in areas with slopes less than 30 percent. Through a regression analysis he confirmed that deer prefer those sites that present a more regular topography. Based on this, the model assumes that the habitats with a slope of less than 30 percent will have double the value of those located in terrain with slopes greater than 30 percent.

Interdistance between habitats. The importance of plant diversity and the juxtaposition of patches of habitats for white-tailed deer have been reported by many investigations. According to Suring and Vohs, white-tailed deer use pastures that are immediately adjacent to forest to a great extent. Williamson and Hirth indicate that the cost to obtain food for the deer will increase when the animal searches for food resources around the center of open areas; therefore, the distance from cover will be greater and will present more exposure to predators.

The model assumes that as distance increases from the edge of the forest toward the center of a pasture, then the probability of use decreases. The size of the home range used for this model (178 ha, average radius of 750 m) was obtained from an average of home ranges for the dry season in different zones of the dry forest on Costa Rica's Pacific side.

Water. The distribution of bodies of water influences the use of habitat by white-tailed deer in the dry season. The evaluation of this variable was based on the average radius of the home range of the species for the dry season (750 m). In this way, four categories were created, where the maximum value was assigned to those areas located at less than 750 m from water (i.e., the resource is available within the average home range).

Vegetation cover for protection. Six categories of cover in each different habitat were calculated using a quantitative field method. With the use of six categories a gradient for coverage was created that assumed that the more horizontal vegetation cover present, the safer the deer from its predators.

Human factors. The combination of the above variables can indicate if a determined habitat is appropriate for the species; however, the presence of small settlements and human activity could negatively affect the deer's use of habitat. The categories used to evaluate this variable are subjective because the true effects of human activity on the deer's behavior have not been evaluated. The model assumes that the species will make the most use of those zones located further away from human presence.

Preliminary Verification of the Model

Through the use of GIS, the map of plot locations was superimposed on the distribution map for HSI values. Next, for each of the sectors where the plots were installed, the average number of feces groups was calculated for that sector (polygon), which corresponds to a determined HSI value. A correlation coefficient was calculated for the HSI values and the average number of feces groups (in 100 m^2), using the statistical tests of Spearman's Coefficient. In order to relate qualitatively the presence of the species to the quality of the habitat, a map of points was designed for those sites with the presence of deer (sightings and signs such as feces and tracks), which was then superimposed on the map of the quality of habitat potential.

Results

According to the developed model, a total of fourteen different HSI values exist for the study area. Based on these values and the presence or absence (limiting factor) of the variables with major importance in the model (water, food, and vegetation cover), seven categories of quality of habitat potential were obtained:

1. High: all factors of well-being for the species are present
2. Medium (food): presents food as the limiting factor
3. Medium (cover): presents vegetation cover as the limiting factor
4. Medium (water): presents water as the limiting factor
5. Low (cover, food): presents food and vegetation cover as the limiting factors
6. Low (cover, water): presents vegetation cover and water as the limiting factors
7. Inappropriate: all factors for well-being are limited.

The results indicate that the majority of the area of study is potentially optimal habitat for white-tailed deer. Approximately 22,500 ha are found in this category, and approximately 50 percent are located in the protected wildlife areas in the zone (Palo Verde National Park and Lomas Barbudal Biological Reserve), with the other half in private farms and government farms of Costa Rica's Instituto de Desarrollo Agrario (IDA, or Institute of Agrarian Reform). Approximately 25 percent (15,810.4 ha) of the total area does not provide minimal conditions for deer (inappropriate habitat). The rest of the 21,891.7 ha have limits in some of the habitat requirements for the species. A preliminary verification of the model indicated a significant correlation between the HSI index and the average number of feces/plot/site ($r_s = 0.64$, d.f. = 44, $p < 0.01$).

Table 10.1. Area of Each Category of Habitat Quality Potential for ***Odocoileus Virginianus*** Present on the Study Area (Bagaces 1994).

Habitat Quality	Area (ha)	Percent
High	21,512.25	35.8
Medium (food)	854.50	1.4
Medium (cover)	9,363.00	15.6
Medium (water)	868.00	1.4
Low (cover, food)	11,633.62	19.4
Low (cover, water)	38.25	0.1
Inappropriate	15,810.44	26.3
Total	60,080.06	100.0

The present model is designed to provide comparisons between different areas at a fixed time or among time periods for a given area. It is not a load capacity model because not all factors that influence animal abundance are included in the model. However, an HSI of 0.9 can indicate better habitat quality than an HSI of 0.48, and it is possible that the former could represent a potentially higher load capacity.

Even though this model did not include other variables of interest (e.g., competition and diseases), it is a tool for decision making in species habitat management. Sites with excellent characteristics for deer are identified (high quality) as are sites with limiting factors for the species (medium, low, and inappropriate quality). One of the potential applications of this model is selection of sites for reintroduction of the species.

Because the medium-quality sites have some limiting habitat requirements, they could be improved with management techniques or simply fulfill other functions equally important for the management and conservation of the species. For example, these habitats can provide buffer for the high-quality habitats and serve as biological corridors that connect high-quality habitats (provided that the vegetation cover is not a limiting factor).

Currently, most efforts in classifying and mapping terrain in order to understand the distribution of habitat requirements of a species are directed toward threatened or endangered species. Halls indicated the necessity of carrying out investigations on common or widespread species, such as this one, since the habitat mapping for species like the white-tailed deer had not been given sufficient importance due to their extensive distributions. With better habitat management techniques, we will be able to prevent common species from becoming rare in the future.

9

Implementation of GIS in Different Sectors

GIS for Electric and Gas

GIS, however, is more than a pretty map. It gives managers insight that improves operations, streamlines work processes, and improves customer service. GIS offers utilities

- A means for outage management response
- A basis for building facilities
- A system for service call and fleet management work
- A resource for market strategizing
- An automation process for every day work tasks
- And more.

With the power of GIS at hand, utility managers can better understand their service area needs and their resources for meeting those needs. GIS is most powerful when utilities integrate it into their information technology infrastructure. This allows utilities to visualize the data through intelligent maps in their multiple systems:

- Customer service
- Supervisory control and data acquisition (SCADA)
- Work management

- Financial
- Human resources

Furthermore, they can capture spatial information on weather intelligence, line clearing cycles, or field service dispatching from outside sources and consolidate it for new decision-making tools. By placing GIS as a core component within the enterprise technology system, company managers can better achieve their business goals.

Utility GIS Solutions

Spatially enabled information can help solve business problems within a utility.

Asset Management

Predictive Maintenance

- Using spatial analysis to find out where problems may exist.
- Using spatial analysis to better schedule and coordinate work.

Corrective Maintenance

- Locate where bad performing assets tend to occur and fix them.

Load Forecasting and Planning

- Using external data sources to find out where new loads may materialize.

Business for Utilities

Business processes are in every department of a utility and can benefit from the integration of GIS analysis and visualization to support decision making and communication.

- Economic Development
- Marketing
- Inventory Management
- Bad Debt Management
- Employee Management
- Fleet Management
- Risk Management

Design

Shorten Design Cycles

- ❐ Lower overall design labor costs.
- ❐ Reduce as-built backlog.
- ❐ Put plant assets "on the books" faster.

Optimize Design

- ❐ Lower overall material costs.
- ❐ Fewer poles, shorter cables.
- ❐ Lower construction labor costs.

Emergency Management

GIS supports the common elements of emergency management:

- ❐ Planning
- ❐ Mitigation
- ❐ Preparation
- ❐ Response
- ❐ Recovery

Generation and Transmission

Facility Site Location

- ❐ Optional paths for transmission routes
- ❐ Selection for solar or wind generation

Asset Management

- ❐ Creating and maintaining asset records
- ❐ Engineering and design of facilities

Maintenance and Inspections

- ❐ Regulatory reporting
- ❐ Optimizing work plans

Environmental Impacts

- ❐ Renewable energy
- ❐ Environmental impact studies

Land Management

In addition to managing energy deliver assets, utilities manage a variety of land assets and activities:

- Permitting
- Rights-of-Way
- Vegetation Management
- Work Area Boundaries
- Tax Boundaries

Other Applications

One Call—Call Before You Dig

- Finds exact location quickly.
- Routes the mark up personnel to the job site.

Inspection and Maintenance—Interfaces With Work Management

- Scheduling
- Routing
- Analysis of problem areas

Joint Use

- Generate additional revenue.

Economic Development

- Advance the quality of life.
- Strengthen the economic base of your community.
- Retain and grow existing businesses.
- Attract new investment.

Outage Management

- GIS links to OMS.
- Connectivity—network model must be maintained.
- ArcGIS has extensive networking facilities.
- Extend the OMS using ArcGIS Schematics.
- Critical customer service and regulatory issues.

Pipeline Management

GIS improves pipeline operators' ability to conduct:

- Engineering and design
- Manage pipeline integrity
- Inspect and maintain facilities

- Meet regulatory compliance

Work Force Productivity

Logistics

- Allows for optimal routing.
- Meets customer appointments.
- Know where your crews are.
- Productivity measurement.
  - Administration time
  - Travel time
  - Actual work time

GIS for Conservation

Global climate change, habitat loss, and human disruptions, such as pollution and deforestation, can cause wildlife fragmentation, extinction and threaten the biodiversity of the earth.

Sustaining biodiversity and preventing fragmentation, extinction, and natural resource depletion are crucial to conservation of the environment. The ability to use GIS technology as a tool to monitor habitat change, track wildlife demographics, and predict future land and resource use is essential to conservation goals and practices. The spatial and thematic aspects of GIS technology enable users to overlay various data to delineate and predict the future of our resources, land, ocean, plant life, and wildlife. This geoprocessing enables decision makers to implement laws and programs that will protect and sustain the environment and its resources.

GIS is a tool that manages, analyzes, and models data from our environment so that we can make decisions based on that information to better conserve its resources and protect its biodiversity.

Woodlands, Wetlands and Watersheds

GIS is a tool that can be used to prevent damage to the valuable resources and habitats of our woodlands, wetlands, and watersheds. Deforestation; loss of biodiversity; and resource depletion due to global climate change, CO_2 emissions, logging, forest fires, and other human disruptions are threats to the earth's woodlands, wetlands, and watersheds. GIS allows users to handle geospatial information to monitor change in targeted areas. Modeling change with GIS permits conservationists to make well-informed decisions about protection plans, reserve policies, and future land-use practices that will most benefit the conservation of forests, biodiversity, wildlife, and resources.

Marine

GIS is used around the world to acquire and manage oceanic data as well as analyze and map marine habitats, water quality, species distribution and population, species behavior, pollution, fishing grounds, and other factors that impact marine life. ESRI 's ArcGIS software suite is a tool that helps visualize and understand areas in danger of biodiversity loss, habitat degradation, and resource depletion. It also aids in monitoring and examining the effectiveness of conservation practices and protected areas to ensure the preservation of the earth's oceans.

Studying Marine Life

Marine wildlife populations are threatened by global warming, extreme weather, natural and man-made pollution, over harvesting, and additional human disturbances. GIS technology manages and analyzes oceanic data, and its temporal and spatial aspects make it an effective instrument for mapping different marine habitats, water quality, species distribution and population, species behavior, pollution, and fishing grounds to show which species are being threatened and what actions can be taken to restore and maintain their populations.

Sustainable Practice

The growing human population and its demands on the earth's resources generate a need for sustainable practices to continue its use of essential, life-supporting resources. The decision to implement sustainable practices often requires collaboration between different organizations; there is frequently a struggle between economically prosperous and environmentally friendly development initiatives. GIS technology bridges the gap between different sectors and acts as a tool to integrate, manage, analyze, and visually format data from multiple sources. The server-based software ArcGIS Server allows users across the globe to share ideas about how to meet their resource needs, plan efficient land-use, and protect the environment to guarantee the survival of future generations.

Landscape

Preserving the earth's natural landscape is often an overlooked aspect of conservation. Humans have influenced the change of the land so much that often its original features are lost. Open spaces, connected ecosystems, and sites of cultural heritage can be lost in the grand scheme of growth and development. GIS works as a tool to monitor these areas and target landscapes in need of conservation.

The Human Footprint

The extent of the human footprint, our species' mark on the earth, is vast. The growing human population has increased the demand for housing materials, clean water, and land for crops and pastures to meet agricultural needs. The size of open space and land untouched by humans diminishes daily. Conservation of open spaces is difficult to balance with the land-use needs of the human population. However, the ability of GIS technology to overlay areas desired for conservation, property lines, and areas that are best used for agricultural purposes gives us the ability to use land more effectively and enables the preservation of open space, limiting the extent of our footprint.

GIS in Fire Planning and Response

GIS technology vastly improves the efficiency of fire operations, including response, planning, and ground command, through a comprehensive understanding of the location of the fire and whether it's a wildfire or property fire. Successful fire operations depend on obtaining information about the location of the fire quickly, establishing priorities, and implementing a response plan.

Response

GIS is used in CAD to rapidly locate and visually display incident locations. CAD selects the closest available response units and, with appropriate data, displays transportation routes for responding equipment. These features become increasingly valuable when multiple incidents begin to occur or when mutual aid units (unfamiliar with the local area) are utilized.

Valuable data about location can be gathered while responding to the incident through GIS—floor plans, hazardous materials, hydrant type, occupancy, and so on. Responding units can also receive information on traffic congestion or best possible route using applications such as the ArcWeb Services Routing Application.

Advanced Vehicle Location

AVL tracking is one of the newest technologies for the emergency response profession. Dispatch managers can track the location of apparatus on a GIS map at the dispatch center in real time using global positioning system (GPS) transponders attached to vehicles. Likewise, responders can visualize their current location in reference to the incident location and manage their response accordingly.

Modeling

Wildfire spread and perimeter location can be modeled in GIS. This helps fire managers predict where a wildfire will be at various times. Wildfire suppression strategies and tactics, as well as the allocation of fire fighting resources to critical locations, can be improved. Fire modeling also presents unique training opportunities for fire suppression personnel.

Planning

GIS is ideal for fire planning. Fire hydrant locations, response area requirements, hazardous material locations, commercial building locations, fire history, station location needs, and other key requirements can be analyzed and visually displayed in GIS.

Wildland fire program planning includes prescribed fire requirements, fire prevention program needs, and initial attack equipment locations. Analyzing vegetation, slope, and other landscape features, GIS becomes the primary tool for all aspects of wildfire program planning.

HAZUS-MH

HAZUS-MH is a nationally applicable standardized methodology and software program that contains models for estimating potential losses from earthquakes, floods, and hurricane winds.

HAZUS-MH was developed by the Federal Emergency Management Agency (FEMA) under contract with the National Institute of Building Sciences (NIBS). Loss estimates produced by HAZUS-MH are based on current scientific and engineering knowledge of the effects of hurricane winds, floods, and earthquakes. Estimating losses is essential to decision-making at all levels of government, providing a basis for developing mitigation plans and policies, emergency preparedness, and response and recovery planning.

HAZUS-MH uses ArcGIS software to map and display hazard data and the results of damage and economic loss estimates for buildings and infrastructure. It also allows users to estimate the impacts of hurricane winds, floods, and earthquakes on built environment and populations. HAZUS-MH is fast-running to facilitate use in real time to support response and recovery following a natural disaster.

Federal, state, and local government agencies and the private sector can order HAZUS-MH free of charge from FEMA.

HAZUS-MH MR2 Now Available

The FEMA Mitigation Division announces the public release of HAZUS-MH Maintenance Release 2 (MR 2).

Earthquake Model

- Optimized Building Damage Module that uses seven combinations of design levels and building quality levels (reduced from nine).
- Technical Manual Chapter 4 guidance for selecting attenuation functions.
- Corrected Wyoming and Montana default mapping schemes.

Hurricane Model

- Availability of mitigation analysis options for all building classes and capability to specify the percentages of each building class that have one or more mitigation features.
- Capability to estimate tree debris weight or volume that is likely to be collected and discarded at public expense.
- Capability through an "Automatic Outputs" tool in the analysis options window to specify a standard set of summary reports and map layers that will be generated after each analysis and automatically exported to the study region folder.
- Capability to generate a range, representing the 5th and 95th percentiles, of potential damage and loss estimates for a given hurricane forecast, based on track and intensity errors in forecast advisories issued during the past 12 years, and to include the results in a new rapid loss summary report.
- Minor adjustments to the Hurricane Model Summary Reports to improve consistency among the three models.

Flood Model

- Capability to create study regions larger than four counties using the full version of SQL Server.
- The Flood Information Tool (FIT), released in 2002, was designed to process and convert locally available flood information to data that can be used by the HAZUS Flood Module. The FIT User Manual provides guidance to users for installing and using the tool effectively within to manipulate flood data into the format required by the HAZUS flood model.
- The Flood Macro Wizard (Flood Wizard) facilitates the preparation of flood risk assessments. The Flood Wizard allows users to automatically process flood data to evaluate exposure and develop loss estimates for the inventory in a study region.

Overview

HAZUS-MH (Multi-Hazards) is a powerful, free ArcGIS extension developed by the Federal Emergency Management Agency under contract with the National Institute of Building Sciences. HAZUS-MH works with ArcGIS Desktop to display hazard data and estimate the impacts of hurricanes, floods, and earthquakes on communities (e.g., damage to buildings and lifelines, estimates of displaced populations and shelter needs, and short- and long-term economic impacts).

HAZUS-MH can be used by individuals and organizations with limited knowledge of hazard analysis, as well as by those with extensive expertise in the earth, building, and GIS sciences due to its diverse range of options. This seminar provides an overview of the capabilities of HAZUS-MH and how it can support mitigation, response, and recovery efforts.

The presenter will discuss:

- Capabilities of HAZUS-MH
- Benefits of using HAZUS-MH
- The Flood, Earthquake, and Hurricane Models and their corresponding outputs
- Additional resources and training opportunities

ArcGIS 9, ArcView 9,ArcGIS 9, ArcEditor 9,ArcGIS 9, ArcInfo 9,HAZUS-MH (Multi-Hazards)

This presentation applies to the following software:

ArcGIS Desktop	**Version**
ArcView	9.0, 9.1 or 9.2
ArcEditor	9.0, 9.1 or 9.2
ArcInfo	9.0, 9.1 or 9.2
Other	**Version**
HAZUS-MH (Multi-Hazards)	MR 2

CATS for Emergency Response

Consequences Assessment Tool Set (CATS) is a PC-based system for powerful, cost-effective disaster analysis.

Before Disaster Strikes

- Create realistic scenarios for training and planning.
- Create contingency plans with CATS comprehensive population and infrastructure data.

When Disaster Strikes

- Assess the affected population quickly and accurately.
- Track hurricane damage.
- Assess damage from earthquake, tidal surge, explosives, industrial agent release, or weapons of mass destruction.
- Reduce response timelines.
- Determine roadblock locations and exclusion zones for safe routing of responders and victims.

After Disaster Strikes

- Assess needs and locate resources for a sustained response.
- Obtain information for reporting, damage assessment, and lessons learned.
- Obtain support for remediation and compensation.

CATS works with ArcView and a wide range of georeferenced background map, population distribution, and infrastructure databases. CATS is easy to use and accepts custom databases to support user specific needs.

Health and Human Services

GIS provides a common analytical framework in which public health authorities can understand problems and formulate a response, improving incident management and health planning.

Most health and human service problems facing the world today exist in a geographic context and any analysis must consider that. Understanding issues ranging from medical epidemiology to healthcare access requires a comprehensive understanding of their geography.

Public Health

GIS is becoming a vital tool for scientists and public health officials investigating the cause and spread of deadly diseases around the world.

Outbreaks of infectious diseases such as SARS can be quickly analyzed using GIS tools. The screen shot above contains a Web site established in Hong Kong to track the locations of reported SARS cases. GIS allowed early recognition that a large multi-story residential complex was a "reservoir" for the infection. The globalization of infectious disease makes the use of GIS critical across the healthcare system in every national health ministry.

GIS Integrates Data

For example

- **Market Data:** Births, Death, Disease, Population Demographics
- **Infrastructure:** Buildings, Roads, Floor Plans, Nursing Units
- **Internal Data:** Product Lines, Patients, Utilization, Revenues
- **Facilities:** Hospitals, Physician Offices, Retail Health Outlets, Employer Locations
- **Administrative Boundaries:** Service Regions, Referral Areas, Planning Areas, Zip, Census
- **Environmental:** Topographic, Bio-Hazards, Toxic Sites, Infectious Disease, Air and Water Quality Testing Sites

Command Center

Managing a public health situation is critical to the reputation of any national health ministry. Assessments must be made quickly and accurately using the best information available.

The command center uses many different GIS applications such as ArcGIS Tracking Server and ArcGIS 3D Analyst to monitor, display, and analyze situations. Data from multiple sources that may include weather information, medical assets, and public health capabilities can be shared to improve response times and lead to better decisions.

Hospitals

Hospital capacity changes continuously. ICU and CCU occupancies fluctuate dramatically, dependent on staffing and physician availability. Knowing real-time capacities for emergency events is essential.

The above screen shot provides an example of GIS linked to an internal Hospital Information System (HIS). With this application, the hospital care location of every patient is linked directly to the clinical events relevant to that patient. Hospitals using GIS can report the exact status of every bed, allowing informed decisions about availability in emergencies. GIS also allows hospital management to see the physical location of each patient within the healthcare environment and to more efficiently allocate resources and speed up admissions.

ESRI software provides solutions designed to work in concert with existing HIS's.

Other GIS Solutions for Hospitals

Hospitals today are using GIS to accomplish a wide variety of important analytical and reporting tasks such as:

- Revenue enhancement
- Facility site location
- Bed surge capacity management
- Trauma analysis
- Home health nurse routing
- Marketing and strategic planning

GIS Integrates Data

For example

- **Market data:** births, death, disease, population demographics
- **Infrastructure:** buildings, roads, floor plans, nursing units
- **Internal data:** product lines, patients, utilization, revenues
- **Facilities:** hospitals, physician offices, retail health outlets, employer locations
- **Administrative boundaries:** service regions, referral areas, planning areas, zip, census
- **Environmental:** topographic, bio-hazards, toxic sites, infectious disease, air and water quality testing sites

Managed Care

Arranging and paying for healthcare is an important activity in any health organization.

GIS provides an efficient way to organize and manage a wide variety of administrative, medical, and social services to patients or clients.

- Home health and social service caseworkers
- Hospital discharge planners
- Disease management
- Lab couriers

Health organizations are using GIS to help their workforce deliver higher client service. Getting clients and workers to the right place efficiently has become a business imperative for most public health, hospital, and human service organizations.

Data Access and Exchange

Mobile GIS provides a sound and secure way to capture data in the field using relatively inexpensive computer devices to accurately collect geographical and health related attributes quickly and with high levels of confidence.

Transforming a public health agencies manual data collection activities into a modern information system environment requires re-engineering the way public health workers capture and transmit information and GIS provides a sound foundation for the collection of data that is spatially relevant. Field authenticated data using ArcPad allows the highest quality of data to become part of a public health authority's information system.

Business Analyst Online for Health

With Business Analyst Online for Health private healthcare providers and hospitals can access presentation-quality reports and maps for use in product planning, market forecasting, and other marketing applications. Reports and maps are based on extensive demographics and consumer data, as well as hospital discharge information, and ICD9 codes, or medical diagnostic codes.

GIS in Law Enforcement

GIS software uses geography and computer-generated maps as an interface for integrating and accessing massive amounts of location-based information. GIS allows law enforcement and criminal justice personnel to effectively plan for emergency response, determine mitigation priorities, analyze historical events, and predict future events. GIS can also be used to get critical information to emergency responders upon dispatch or while en route to an incident to assist in tactical planning and response.

Law enforcement agencies face a multitude of tasks and challenges in their daily responsibility of protecting life and property while keeping the peace in their communities. Virtually every task and challenge has a geographic component. These tasks require both strategic and tactical planning in rapidly changing social, economic, and political environments. While law enforcement agencies collect vast amounts of data, only a very small part of this information can be absorbed from spreadsheets and database files. GIS provides a visual, spatial means of displaying data, allowing law enforcement agencies to integrate and leverage their data for more informed decision making.

GIS is the next step in the evolution of information technology. It is a core information and analysis tool that helps manage not only geographic data but other data sets as well. GIS has been embraced by professionals in all areas of law enforcement for conducting day-to-day operations as well as for planning, analysis and decision support.

Law Enforcement and the GIS Enterprise

Law enforcement benefits from enterprise GIS by making critical information from local, state, and federal government agencies easily accessible. By integrating information such as property ownership, accessible streets and highways, hazardous material locations, fire preplans, zoning information, law enforcement administrators can plan and react more effectively.

Crime and Investigative Analysis

Crime mapping provides a valuable spatial element to crime analysis. GIS maps traditional statistical information used in crime analysis, revealing crime patterns and relationships. By looking at non emergency service calls and non criminal incidents on a map, you can make better decisions on how and where to place resources.

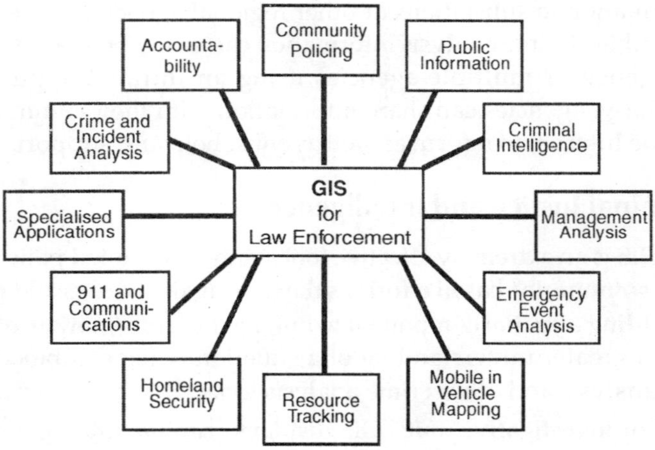

You can use GIS for predictive modeling to manage field assignments and investigative efforts. GIS analysis of traffic data assists in the identification of selective enforcement locations.

For example, ArcGIS Spatial Analyst helps you examine locations of citation issuance against accident locations, types of citations issued, accidents involving impaired drivers, and other issues.

Community Policing and Public Information

GIS enables agencies to employ traditional community policing methods to identify and respond to nontraditional issues such as the potential relationship between neighborhood blight or school dropout rates and juvenile-related offenses.

Combining multiple datasets in a GIS can have a powerful effect in focusing local resources to address community needs. You can integrate and analyze data such as

- Demographics (neighborhood profiles)
- Housing
- Types of businesses (liquor stores, adult entertainment) and their relationship to incidents

- School drop-out rates
- Evaluate locations for community policing services

ArcIMS Internet/Intranet capabilities enable an agency to serve information to substations or other regional agencies as well as to the public. Crime analysis information can easily be shared within an agency or multiple agencies using an Intranet application. Similarly, agencies can share information with their communities via the Internet to inform as well as enlist help and support.

Criminal Justice and Intelligence

GIS is an extremely effective tool in intelligence-led policing for such community-based efforts as the fight against drugs and gangs. By adding a spatial component to intelligence information, officers gain a greater understanding of a situation when combined with link analysis and other crime analysis tools.

For investigative units, GIS displays criminal intelligence and crime analysis information graphically with both mapping and link analysis capability. GIS allows prosecutors offices to serve subpoenas and summonses more effectively through the use of automated routing software such ArcLogistics Route. Intranet/Internet capability enables offices to serve this information to satellite offices and/or other agencies.

Prosecutors and public defenders use GIS to map filing locations and workloads to determine office sitting and geographic areas of responsibility. It also enables them to provide interactive mapping presentations, including photographs, video, fingerprints, and documents, to dramatically improve case preparation and presentation.

Corrections, Parole and Probation

GIS helps corrections officers determine potential facility sites by examining complex, seemingly unrelated criteria and displaying them all in a graphical, layered, spatial interface or map.

Officials are using GIS to map inmate populations, fixtures, and equipment to provide for the safety of inmates by separating gang members, identifying high-risk or potentially violent inmates, and identifying hazardous locations in a facility. It can also help to reduce the potential for internal violence by providing better command and control. Criminal intelligence information, including photographs, fingerprints, and documents can be included in this interactive graphical interface.

Intranet/Internet capability enables the information to be shared within and between institutions. GIS "live map" functions, when combined with capabilities of location identification devices (GPS, personal inertial guidance, etc.), facilitate tracking the movement of high-risk inmates or at-risk personnel throughout any facility or area.

GIS use in parole and probation activities means providing analysis through client mapping. It allows an agency to provide better, more efficient workload distribution based upon user-defined criteria. Automated routing can provide a "best route" solution for an officer making residence checks or performing related activities. This saves hours of preparation time each week, enabling the agency to reduce lead time for route planning and to monitor the cost per visit including fleet costs.

Management Analysis and GeoAccounting

Police managers are constantly wrestling with the dilemma of meeting ever-increasing demands for services with stable or decreasing resources. GIS provides the tools and analysis capability to quickly address issues that speak directly to service delivery such as

- Improved response time and performance
- More effectively managed resources
- Improved productivity
- Better workload distribution

For example, managers can routinely examine their workload geographically as well as temporally so they can quickly redistrict police service areas or beats for maximum effectiveness.

Many agencies have engaged in a process to increase accountability among their management, supervisory, and line personnel. GIS is central to this effort. This process has a variety of forms and names including COMSTAT, CAM, ACUDAT, COMSTAC, FASTRAC, and many others.

This process of GIS-based GeoAccounting focuses on determining if the agency, area, or beat crime/incident information is accurate and timely; if the response was focused, coordinated, and rapid; what tactics were employed and what their level of effectiveness was; and, finally, if there is continuing follow-up by command staff to determine whether activities were carried out throughout the organization and, specifically, by field personnel.

Resource Tracking and Management

GIS helps you access and process information quickly. You can deploy resources more effectively to save lives and to maintain the peace. GIS provides law enforcement officers with the capability of automated vehicle location (AVL) for all patrol vehicles, aircraft, and watercraft. This information is crucial in determining the closest officer to a call, in day-to-day tactical considerations such as creating a perimeter to apprehend a subject and, most important, for officer safety.

Use Mobile GIS technology to share valuable data about location while responding to an incident. Responding units can also receive information on traffic congestion or best possible route using applications such as the ArcWeb Services Routing Application.

Vital information, such as the vehicle's current location, whether specialized weapons have been released from their electronic locks, and whether the vehicle is stopped or moving, can be monitored by communications personnel. In addition, fixed assets can be mapped and identified with GIS to provide a better geographic orientation to all department personnel.

Mobile/In-Vehicle Mapping

Both police and communications personnel have long believed that the best response to a call is an informed response. GIS provides the capability to put valuable, potentially life-saving information in the hands of first responders while en route to a call.

Mobile GIS technology gives agencies the ability to easily be share mission critical information between the command center and responders in the field. Officers, supervisors, and managers can understand where each vehicle and person is in relation to the incident, perimeter, or other potential hazards.

GIS gives responding officers local maps, school or business floor plans, locations of high-risk sex offenders, and many other types of critical information at their fingertips on mobile data computers in their vehicles.

GIS provides law enforcement aviation with the capability for in flight real-time maps and automated vehicle location (AVL) for all patrol vehicles, aircraft, and watercraft.

Emergency/Event Management

One of the most important responsibilities of government is providing for the safety and security of its citizens and the community. In this effort, law enforcement agencies struggle daily to match scarce resources with an ever-increasing volume of calls for service.

The challenges facing law enforcement today include the traditional notion of "protecting" and "serving" but also include nontraditional approaches centered in community policing and new tasks oriented to homeland security. To this end, technology plays an important role in assisting the law enforcement community in understanding the issues to meet its obligations.

GIS is instrumental in assisting with many different strategic and tactical problems such as warrant services, SWAT incidents, domestic terrorism, search and rescue operations, disasters, court presentations, and others. During an event or disaster, GIS is a valuable medium for quickly sharing information and improving the decision making process (situational awareness).

ESRI GIS being is used to help manage major sporting events, presidential conventions, civil disturbances, earthquakes, hurricanes, toxic spills, and a myriad of other problems. It is used not only to respond to an emergency event, but in planning, mitigation, preparedness, and post event recovery.

All emergencies, whether caused by nature or people, begin locally and elevate to county, regional, state or national levels depending on severity, complexity, size and the nature of the event. During these events law enforcement managers need the right information at the right time to deploy resources, implement plans (tactical, emergency, evacuation, and so forth), establish medical or other aid, and to manage events as they unfold.

Location-Based Services in GIS

GIS keeps mobile resources safe and keeps you informed of real-time, location-based workflow events for a more productive business.

Efficiency, productivity, time, and cost savings how will you meet these demands? CIOs and IT managers around the globe have turned to ESRI software and Web services for the tools and services to build applications for field-force safety and workflow productivity.

With ESRI, you can run a more productive business by knowing when, where, and how quickly jobs get done. With ESRI, you can build location-based applications for sales force automation, field service automation, and field force automation.

- Route your workers correctly
- Meet customers appointments
- Know where your staff is at all times
- Integrate mobile location into short messaging alert notifications and e-mail
- Communicate more effectively
- Measure and audit mobile workforce productivity
  - Administration time
  - Travel time
  - ·Actual work time

Mobile Government

Emergency 9-1-1, public works, homeland security, and other community services require you to know where your mobile workers are so you can direct them more efficiently. Serve the public better by equipping mobile staff with essential knowledge to act quickly during administrative activities and emergencies.

ESRI software and Web services help you build applications that link your IT framework to mobile locations, maps, routes, and geographic events that help you and your staff communicate and respond more effectively.

- Serve e-9-1-1 callers
- Respond to public works problem reports
- Inform mobile crews of changing emergency conditions

- Integrate mobile location into short messaging alert notifications and e-mails

Mobile Developer

With ESRI software tools and Web services, you can location-enable any Web, mobile Internet, messaging, J2ME, CE, or BREW application. ESRI's application servers and Web services help you turn your ideas into practical or profitable solutions.

Pipeline Facilities

AM/FM GIS or a hybrid GIS/CAD system can greatly reduce the time and money required to update alignment sheets.

Competitive pressure and regulatory constraints are placing increasing demands on pipeline operators to operate in an efficient and responsible manner. Responding to these demands requires accessibility to information regarding geographically distributed assets and operations.

GIS technology facilitates the organization and management of data with a geographic component. It also eases data acquisition and utilization. GIS provides the pipeline operator with improved capability to manage pipeline integrity, improved efficiencies in pipeline operations, and improved response to business development opportunities.

GIS for Risk Management

GIS-based risk evaluation provides a comprehensive, systematic method for building and maintaining comprehensive pipeline risk models and supporting risk mitigation, emergency response, remediation, reporting, and investigation.

ESRI's GIS technology provides the data integration capabilities, modeling tools, analytical functionality, and graphical reporting environment necessary to build and maintain comprehensive pipeline risk models and attribute risk to sections of a pipeline for prioritization of upgrade and maintenance. GIS software from ESRI facilitates the building of an integrated system for

- Formulating predictive queries for identification of potential high-risk areas

- Utilizing risk assessment data as a base for failure management
- Modeling failure analysis to enhance risk assessment and maintenance programs
- Scenario building for development of emergency response, mitigation, and remediation plans
- Ensuring use of current operational data for safer, more efficient field operations
- Generating reports for improved communication and support of due diligence

Disciplined maintenance and use of the risk management system fosters

- Reduction of lost revenues due to failure and costs associated with remediation
- Processes to ensure regulatory compliance and due diligence
- Management of risks associated with operational activities
- Maintenance of a broad perspective regarding the emergence and mitigation of risks
- Reduction of uncertainty and liability associated with energy production and transportation

GIS for Route Planning and Construction

Optimal planning of a large-scale pipeline development project requires integration of the geographic information governing the engineering, environmental, and socioeconomic costs. Use of GIS technology for data management and analysis provides the most effective method for defining these complex geographical relationships and for computing optimal solutions to these multivariate problems.

Using Satellite Technology to Enhance Route Analysis Process

Global satellites continuously collect in-depth information about activities and conditions in every country. These satellite data offer critical insights into cultural and physical conditions that affect the planning and construction of large, complex pipeline projects. Information such as land use, geology and soils, hazards, development, and environmentally sensitive areas can be extracted from satellite imagery, providing accurate and timely data at varying levels of detail.

The satellite data can be integrated with other data sets, such as political and socioeconomic information, to build feasibility and risk models for the extensive geographic areas often involved in pipeline construction. The result is a more efficient, higher-confidence route planning process. Key characteristics include

- Rapid, comprehensive data collection
- Flexible, accurate analysis
- Improved risk modeling and scenario building
- Improved defensibility and communication of decisions
- Flexibility to incorporate revision into the route planning process

Construction

GIS technology for pipeline construction can be used to perform these and other tasks:

- Assisting surveyors in making route adjustments to minimize impact on sensitive or problem areas.
- Locating optimum access roads, staging and fueling locations, work camps, and so forth.
- Identifying areas prone to forest fire or soil erosion or areas where the impact of air, noise, or water pollution may be significant.
- Identifying periods of low flow rate for scheduling of water crossings.
- Locating a water crossing at a point that minimizes damage to the bank and river bed will ease both construction costs and environmental impact.
- Identifying watercourse banks and beds that could be damaged by heavy equipment or skidding of logs.
- Erosion management on slopes and watercourses and slope analysis to determine erosion control structures required.

- Identifying sensitive ecological periods to avoid disruptions such as wildlife migration or fish spawning.
- Identifying normal industrial or agricultural activity to avoid disruptions such as irrigation and harvest season or log hauling.
- Assisting in contingency planning and allowing for quick modification of emergency response to adapt to specific incidents. Examples are fire fighting, spill response, or sedimentation of aquatic habitats.
- Capturing and managing data (collected by survey crews or construction personnel) regarding potential or actual construction problems, sensitive soils, wildlife habitat, and heritage sites.
- Identifying timber that can be harvested from aerial survey and/or ground survey.
- Developing harvest plan.
- Planning of trenching to avoid blocking movement of wildlife, livestock, vehicle traffic, draining swamps, diverting water flow, and causing sedimentation of aquatic habitats.
- Aerial analysis (area of right-of-way) to determine area requiring revegetation.
- Capturing essential information on construction materials and equipment. For example, each weld can be precisely located in *x, y, z* coordinates using GPS. Attributes of the weld such as welder name, weather conditions, welding rod type, and others can be recorded in association with the location. Information about each pipe section can be recorded and associated with its adjoining welds. Bar-coded pipe, which provides a history of the pipe from ingot through the pipe mill, provides an effective way to correlate corrosion statistics with pipe characteristics.

GIS for Supply and Market Analysis

GIS technology is used extensively for customer analysis in the retail and service industries. As in these industries, pipeline users can use GIS to determine the most suitable location for distribution points based on parameters such as demographics, transportation networks, zoning, and real estate costs. Energy usage statistics can be mapped, grouped, and overlaid with existing pipeline data to determine the feasibility for direct delivery of gas to large industrial gas users.

GIS is also is being used for supply analysis. GIS is used extensively by most major upstream oil and gas organizations as a data management and analysis tool for exploration, production, and land analysis. The data that are available from the upstream division of an integrated oil company can be invaluable to the pipeline division both as a means to establish base maps from which to work and as a means to perform analysis for supply. Certain types of analyses, such as forecasting decline in reserves, tie in to new developments. Mapping of gas/oil ratios can show the potential of oil reservoirs to become excellent sources for gas supply. Using GIS as a means to monitor drilling activity, development of supply sources, proximity of supply to competitor pipelines, and for construction cost analysis can enhance the available supply and supply reliability.

GIS can be used to model supply points, delivery points, and pipeline interconnects. GIS network tracing and analysis can then be used to determine product routing optimizing for parameters such as line capacity and tariff structures. GIS can provide data management and reporting support for sophisticated product transaction management systems.

GIS for Petroleum

Discovering new sources of petroleum ahead of the competition is one of the key ways to staying successful in the petroleum industry. A GIS can help you evaluate the potential for oil in promising locations.

Exploration often requires analysis of satellite imagery, digital aerial photo mosaics, seismic surveys, surface geology studies, subsurface and cross section interpretations and images, well locations, and existing infrastructure information. A GIS can relate these data elements to the location in question in map form and allow you to overlay, view, and manipulate the data to analyze and understand their potential.

GIS technology today allows us to manage the spatial components of these everyday petroleum "business objects," such as leases, wells, pipelines, environmental concerns, facilities, and retail outlets, in the corporate database, and apply appropriate geographic analysis efficiently in a desktop-focused application.

GIS for Facilities Management

Managing Facilities Worldwide

The global nature of the petroleum industry results in an infrastructure that is vast and difficult to manage. A large, integrated oil company must keep track of everything from drilling platforms to pipeline networks to refineries. The commercial, operational, and often harsh environmental conditions in which these facilities exist make it critical that they be planned, operated, and maintained effectively. Often, finding an economic reserve is as much dependent on a practically and properly implemented facilities structure as it is on the exploration and production itself. Certainly the profitability of a commercial venture is often heavily dependent on the facility and pipeline infrastructure. GIS can be used to map the gathering and transmission of products to a facility. Once there, integrating with more traditional "in plant" infrastructure management systems, such as CAD, attribute records, and scanned documents, allows the true geographic placement of CAD entities complementing the CAD architecture.

GIS for Retail Planning

Like businesses in most industries, the question of where to place a retail outlet must be answered carefully to ensure the site reaches its full sales potential.

Companies such as Texaco use GIS to analyze demographic and transportation information to effectively choose retail sites and build outlets tailored to the anticipated customer segment. They can also use the technology to analyze customer receipts for stores to adjust the store profile and stock.

GIS for Surveying

Surveyors and engineers understand the importance of geographic data. Surveyors use precise instruments, procedures, and computations to accurately locate and define geographic features while conducting field surveys that range from cadastral to engineering construction layout. Engineers design and build structures and infrastructures on geography measured by surveyors.

Research/Reconnaissance

With GIS, you can easily research land records, parcel data, legal documents, and additional data needed from courthouses and online data warehouses to begin a new project.

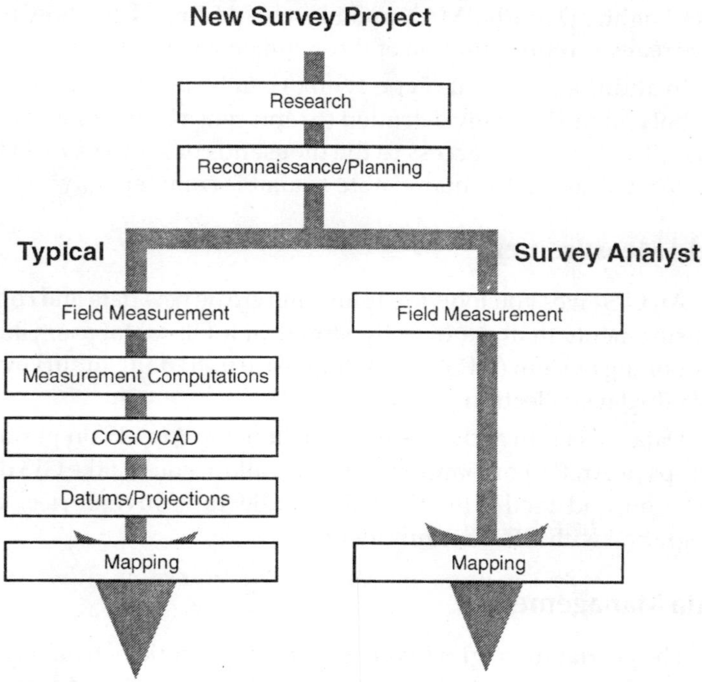

Advanced GIS technologies such as Survey Analyst provide interfaces and integration of survey data. Because survey accurate measurements establish the legal definition of a parcel, this capability is essential in the accuracy of land records and assessment data. Even as new, more accurate data is collected, GIS has the capability to adjust existing data to conform to new survey measurements while preserving the spatial integrity of the land records geodatabase.

Reconnaissance

Brass tops, witness trees, rocks, and iron rods are types of monuments called by surveyors to be re-used as control points in future surveys. You will find over 500 industry-standard three-dimensional symbols included with ArcGIS 3D Analyst. These symbols can be used to represent GIS features, such as trees or fire hydrants for point features, grass or water for polygon features, and tubes or texture lines for line features. ArcGIS 3D Analyst supports specialized three-dimensional models, including MultiGen OpenFlight, 3D Studio MAX and SketchUp formats, to allow for a more realistic representation of three-dimensional features.

In addition, any TrueType symbol can be used as a base for a symbol and can be easily extruded to represent a three-dimensional object. This gives you access to the thousands of symbols included with ArcGIS as well as many more available commercially.

Field Measurement

ArcGIS gives you tools to capture and create new data and collect measurements that are directly stored in a GIS database. Global Positioning System (GPS) technologies are used daily in surveying and GIS data collection.

Data collection activities in the field using ArcGIS on portable laptops or ArcPad on handheld devices allow you to take GIS data with you and facilitates field data collection, inventories, and integration with GPS measurements.

Data Management

The geodatabase gives you the ability to handle rich data types and apply sophisticated rules and relationships. In addition to managing large volumes of geographic data, it also implements sophisticated business logic that, for example, builds relationships between data types, such as topologies and geometric networks, validates data, and controls access.

Data management tools scale to meet your needs, from the individual to workgroups and large, multi-user, enterprises. Direct support is included for a wide variety of standard vector and raster sources, and includes data import and export utilities to support many other formats. These capabilities provide for integration and interoperability with many other products, and offer complete flexibility in work flow support.

Computation/Analysis

GIS technology gives you the tools to develop geodetic data that is compliant and provides the surveying, GIS, and mapping communities access to control data derived by state, federal, tribal, local governments, and private companies. Geodetic control can be used for a variety of public and private imagery, mapping, surveying, and construction projects, and also supports spatial accuracy improvement for national mapping frameworks.

The ArcGIS Geostatistical Analyst extension provides a variety of tools for spatial data exploration, identification of data anomalies, optimum prediction, evaluation of prediction uncertainty, and surface creation.

With ArcGIS Tracking Analyst you can play back historical data, use rule-based drawing and see temporal patterns in data. In addition, you can visualize complex time series and spatial patterns and interactions while integrating all other GIS data within the ArcGIS system.

Using ArcGIS Spatial Analyst, you can derive new information from your existing data, analyze spatial relationships, and build spatial models integrating core ArcGIS Desktop and ArcGIS Spatial Analyst tools.

Mapping and Visualization

Measurements, survey points, and computations are all managed and stored in a GIS system. Raw survey data, COGO measurements, and field sketches can be entered directly into the GIS.

You can use GIS software and technology for collecting, importing, converting, and storing spatial measurement and computational fabrics for agencies and private businesses of any size. Also, you can integrate computations (COGO, least squares, etc.) and pre-existing networks, as well as import spatial database classes and relationships

ArcGIS 3D Analyst provides extensive tools to visualize geographic vector or raster data in three dimensions. You can easily drape your data over the terrain; use attributes, such as elevation, to display the data at a preset height; or use attributes to extrude the data.

ArcScan for ArcGIS simplifies the data automation process by providing the method and tools to clean up scanned paper maps and vectorize lines and polygons.

Use ArcScan for ArcGIS to:

- Automate the conversion of scanned paper maps to vector form.
- Reduce the time and expense in creating GIS data.
- Eliminate the tedious need to digitize the data by hand.
- Easily clean up scanned maps.

ArcGIS Publisher adds easy and cost-effective map publication capabilities to ArcGIS. Use ArcGIS Publisher to create published map files (.pmf) from any ArcMap document (.mxd). Published maps can be viewed using any ArcGIS Desktop product, including the no-cost ArcReader application, allowing you to freely share your maps with a wide range of users.

GIS for Transportation

DOTs and Roadway Management

The gateway to economic development and, subsequently, a healthy economy, transportation infrastructure represents one of the largest and most critical investments made in any nation, at any stage of development. Similarly, for many firms in the transportation industry, profitability and a strong competitive position depend on a safe and reliable system.

ESRI's integrated software solutions are being used for analysis and support throughout the infrastructure life cycle.

- Evaluate alternative pavement treatment strategies on the desktop.
- Integrate GIS with other tools such as CAD or document management software.
- Integrate information from real-time traffic devices like cameras and loop detectors for congestion and incident

management.

- Review and coordinate construction projects.
- Visualize output from popular transportation planning models.

Planning

Cube for ArcGIS—the best of transportation planning with the best of GIS. Citilabs and ESRI have worked together to produce a new travel forecasting system integrating Citilabs' advanced modeling techniques with ArcGIS.

Design

Many engineering organizations are advancing the concept of context-sensitive design, recognizing the many factors and multidisciplinary nature required for complex design. In order to extend context-sensitive design practices and to perform a broad range of analyses, engineers need several kinds of tools including databases, surface and hydraulic models, computer-aided design (CAD), and GIS.

Safety and Security

GIS technology can be used to analysis, report, and share up-to-date information quickly with multiple agencies. Highway agencies have also taken on a key role in emergency management by planning and supporting critical functions such as evacuations due to severe weather and natural disasters as well as terrorist and other criminal threats.

The analytical capabilities of GIS support a variety of tasks.

- Crash location and reporting
- Incident and response management
- Accident analysis and "hot spot" identification
- Safety engineering and capital improvement
- Construction site management
- Vulnerability assessment
- Evacuation planning
- Flood and snow emergency operations

- Hazardous material tracking
- Bridge rating and oversize truck permitting
- Lighting and visibility

Railroads

Railways around the world rely on GIS to manage key information for rail operations, maintenance, asset management, and decision support systems. GIS has been successfully deployed in railway organizations for a variety of major functions and disciplines such as

- Real estate management
- Facility management
  - Track
  - Power
  - Communications and signaling
- Asset tracking
- Commodity flow analysis
- Emergency response management
- Environmental and construction management
- Intermodal management
- Passenger information
- Capacity planning
- Marketing
- Supply chain management
- Site selection
- Risk management

Infrastructure

Infrastructure management and maintenance planning involves constantly monitoring a variety of networks such as

- Bridges, tunnels, and track networks
- Communications and signaling networks
- Electric power distribution networks
- Rail yards and other campus facilities

With ArcGIS Schematics, you can create and visualize schematic representations from any linear network so you can check network connectivity, optimize design, and monitor the quality and status of your networks. You also have the power to perform modeling, simulation, and comparative analysis.

GIS also helps you track and manage infrastructure investments and plans in conjunction with real estate management (i.e., valuation maps and lease and tenant management).

Safety and Security

To effectively manage emergency situations (i.e., crime, accidents, spills) GIS gives you immediate access to local data such as

- streets and at-grade crossings
- police, fire, and rescue contact information
- schools
- hospitals
- rivers, streams, and other geographic features

Intermodal Systems

Transporting cargo by rail includes shipping, roadway, and aviation networks. GIS can help manage shipments and transfers more effectively by providing accurate and timely information.

ArcGIS Network Analyst gives you the ability to combine multiple transportation networks for routing shipments more efficiently, saving time and money. GIS also supports the development of "executive dashboards" that bring the benefits of spatial information and intuitive map graphics directly to facility and operations managers.

Passenger Railroads

Communicating with customers and improving rail services brings an added dimension to rail operations. Perform ridership analysis with GIS to coordinate schedules with local bus services and to help place stations relevant to where people live and work.

Real-time tracking systems and Web interfaces let passengers know when a train will arrive for better planning and coordination with other trip details.

GIS for Mass Transit/Public Transport

GIS helps transit operators make safe, reliable decisions based on real information. GIS can be used to manage and analyze critical information such as

- Route planning and analysis
- Bus dispatch and emergency response
- Automatic vehicle location and tracking
- Paratransit scheduling and routing
- Bus stop and facility inventory
- Rail system facility management
- Track, power, communications, and signal maintenance
- Accident reporting and analysis
- Demographic analysis and route restructuring
- Ridership analysis and reporting
- Transportation planning and modeling

Aviation

Airports around the world plan for and manage their facilities by integrating GIS with many other information technology tools. Missions as diverse as security and environmental compliance are served effectively by GIS analysis.

Air traffic control organizations use GIS for both its 2D and 3D capabilities to maintain safe flight paths and efficient re-routing when severe weather conditions interfere with normal operations. Airline and airfreight firms utilize GIS for many activities including facilities management and capacity planning.

Airports

For many years, airport managers have turned to geographic information system (GIS) technology to support their efforts in planning, operations, maintenance, and security by adding spatial information and modeling. GIS provides unique information and analytical capabilities not available in other information systems.

Commercial, emergency, and defense-related airfields use GIS to:

- Manage facilities, both airside and landside.
- Model and monitor noise.
- Facilitate environmental compliance.
- Manage construction and maintenance.
- Improve airside parking operations.
- Plan traffic and capacity.

Airlines

GIS is an excellent tool to support airline management because it is an inherently integrating technology that supports data sharing and analyses across departmental boundaries. A GIS system allows real-time data to be easily shared and utilized for critical operations such as

- Facilities management.
- Capacity planning and business expansion.
- Safety and security.
- Weather and emergency response.

Air Freight

Air freight firms have exhibited several profitable uses for GIS.

- Facility Management
- Supply-chain Analysis
- Capacity Planning
- Site Security
- Ground Delivery Route Analysis
- Weather Alerts and Rerouting Options

Air Traffic Management

A number of air traffic management organizations utilize GIS in areas such as

- Aeronautical chart development.

- Airspace management and permitting.
- Capacity planning.
- Environmental compliance assessment.
- Flight tracking.
- Weather routing and contingency planning.

Production Line Tool Set

The Production Line Tool Set (PLTS) is a commercial off-the-shelf (COTS) software designed to manage, build, and maintain digital databases and hardcopy map products in a production environment. PLTS leverages the object-relational ArcGIS Desktop technology and provides next generation functionality-rich software that streamlines the production process.

Water Transportation

GIS is an important technology tool that manages and analyzes timely information effectively and efficiently for use in a number of key areas. GIS allows for data integration in a way that facilitates understanding and improved decision making.

In addition, many water bodies are extremely sensitive to pollutants and excessive traffic. GIS helps engineers and planners accommodate design goals and environmental constraints more easily. Local models can be developed which provide a glimpse at the potential impact of traffic growth or new construction.

PLTS Nautical Solution is used for high-volume production and maintenance of standard Digital Nautical Chart databases from a variety of sources. Nautical Solution includes desktop production tools to efficiently create and maintain National Geospatial-Intelligence Agency VPF DNC compliant data as well as the Harbor Approach and Coastal chart cartographic product.

Motor Vehicles Administration

Motor vehicle administrators work with a great deal of information that is continuously changing. GIS-based applications can help make sense of the information in your databases by pinpointing critical locations and identifying trends.

Spatial analysis of safety factors, such as congestion, construction zones, and weather, reveal patterns that can be missed in simple tabular or statistical output. Combining digital maps with up-to-date data from accident and moving violation databases can speed the recognition of troublesome hot spots and lead to better solutions.

In addition, the "motor carrier" department can use GIS tools to highlight trends, such as increases in over-dimensional and hazardous materials traffic, permit violations, fuel/mileage tax trends, and general commercial traffic route information.

Intelligent Transportation System (ITS)

GIS: The World's ITS Backbone

The Intelligent Transportation System (ITS) market is one of the world's most diverse in terms of participant types, technologies deployed, and project goals.

ITS uses computer and telecommunication technologies to help unsnarl downtown traffic jams in Tokyo; improve rural road safety in Colorado; speed toll-paying and snow-clearing in northern Virginia; improve public transportation in Florida; ease trucking slowdowns from Canada to the Mexican border; and provide a plethora of in-vehicle services for commuters, commercial carriers, and travelers.

Incident Management and Emergency Response

GIS can be integrated with other systems (e.g., CCTV-Video and VMS) to provide a responsive, ergonomic, and intuitive interface for incident management staff. This is critical for high-stress and extended shift positions, especially during the emergency period. Extended weather emergencies, unusual traffic activity, and security-related events require adaptive and easy-to-use tools.

Distribution and Fleet Management

Efficient operations require accurate, timely decision making. Knowing where a vehicle, pickup, or delivery is at any given time leverages assets for optimum deployment and cost savings. GIS can provide this critical information. Customer satisfaction, competitive position, timely response, effective deployment, and profitability all stand to gain. The matrix below shows a series of basic questions a fleet manager might ask in the course of deciding on a tactical deployment plan or during a strategic review of his or her business. Next to each question is an application or capability of ESRI software that fleet managers can use to answer the question.

Question	Function	Application
Where are my trucks?	Vehicle Tracking	Dispatch
Where is my customer?	Geocoding	Customer Address Matching
How do I get there?	Network Topology	Routing and Scheduling
Where have the trucks been?	Route Logging	Post Trip Analysis, Fuel Tax Mileage Reporting
What is my potential demand?	Accessibility to Customer	Site Selection
Service from a proposed warehouse?	Order Fulfillment	Customer Service Job Pricing

Facilities and Depot Management

GIS by ESRI supports fleet and logistics management with a wide array of software and applications, ranging from planning facility investments and sophisticated location-allocation capabilities to solving various gravity modeling problems.

Fleet management activities for vehicles and depots include the following topics:

- Location
- Capacity
- Inventory
- Range

Route Analysis

Transportation professionals can use GIS to integrate mapping analysis into decision support for everything from calculated arrival times to customer sites and schedule requests. GIS can be used to analyze

- Addresses

- Orders
- History
- "Expedites"

Routing and Scheduling

Through the use of GIS and spatial database systems, fleet managers have enjoyed improved efficiencies in a number of areas.

- Reduced mileage
- Less overtime
- Better schedule adherence
- Higher customer satisfaction
- More "first trip" job completions
- Better asset yield
- More stops per day
- Better directions
- Streamlined route-planning process

Warehouse Operations

Just as vehicles can be more efficiently routed over streets and highways, forklifts and other equipment can be routed for "picks and puts" with greater efficiency. You can use GIS to create a "street" database of the warehouse aisles and assign "address ranges" to shelves, parts bins, and other storage locations. By using GIS to analyze spatial patterns and seasonal variations, you can improve space utilization, saving time and resources.

GIS can also be used to tie the pick order system to the schedules database. This allows warehouse operations to more closely approach the "just-in-time" ideal without leaving material or merchandise near the dock for long periods of time where damage or loss can occur.

GIS for Sustainable Development

GIS software helps organizations, agencies, and governments work together to develop strategies for sustainable development. It provides the tools to access and process information from a variety of sources and display it in a spatial and visual medium.

This supports decision making and promotes better organizational integration and knowledge management to improve the quality of life for future generations.

The Earth Charter

The Earth Charter Commission was formed by the United Nations to oversee a project dedicated to establishing fundamental principals for sustainable development. GIS technology has long played a key role in assisting organizations throughout the world to work together to meet the goals set forth in the charter.

Collecting and interpreting large volumes of data, impact assessments from human development, and disaster recovery efforts are examples of how GIS supports sustainable development on multiple levels.

The Community of Life

GIS technology is used to analyze and better understand the basis for human socioeconomic systems. This includes organizing and describing the volumes of data associated with the Earth's diversity (i.e., climate, soils, vegetation, animals, and human cultures) as ideas, images, and maps. Understanding and sharing such information are integral parts of the respect and care of the community of life.

Visit the industries and programs below to see how each implements GIS technology to describe and gain a better appreciation of the relationships between cultures and their respective natural resources.

GIS for Agriculture

Regardless of scale, whether at the subfield level analyzing crop yield information or internationally assisting governmental organizations with commodity subsidy programs, GIS will become commonplace in the information technologies domain.

Agribusiness Inputs and GIS

Farmers need many inputs to successfully produce agricultural products for sale. A network of local farm supply outlets form the backbone of this supply chain. These farm inputs vary from seed, fertilizer, and agrochemicals to machinery parts; services are also often sold from the same location such as crop insurance and farm credits. How are the crop input manufacturers and service providers to benefit from GIS? Below is a selection of applications where GIS is being used to successfully increase operational efficiency while guaranteeing the best possible service for customers.

Insurance Claim Assessment Using Handheld Field GIS

At any one time there are hundreds of insurance claim agents visiting areas of farmland to ascertain the degree of damage to agricultural products. These personal visits serve two main purposes, first to validate the details of a filed insurance claim, and second to relate procedures related to the claim directly to the farmer. Field data collection, or more precisely, the mapping of damaged areas within a field can only be enhanced by the application of a handheld GIS solution. Available on Windows CE handheld computers, ArcPad gives claim agents the ability to not only interactively map features but also to upload them via the Internet. The ability of ArcPad to load satellite or aerial imagery greatly helps in damage delineation of crops caused by such events as flooding, gales, or hail. If additional processing is required at the farm location, the data can seamlessly be transferred to a laptop with ArcView installed. Once done, a calculation based on the extent of damage can be delivered directly to the farmer. Should it be necessary, the agent is then able to rapidly update this claim information directly to the head office ArcSDE data server via ArcIMS for further approval and confirmation.

The automation of this process works both in favor of the farmer and the insurance company. By using the ArcIMS Internet link, information that exists at the head office can be downloaded, and any queries arising can be straightened out directly with the farmer during the visit. Additional data available might include historical information on previous claims by the client or the most recently acquired satellite imagery for the area under investigation.

One of the most difficult challenges an insurance underwriter faces is in paying its claims. Just how accurate are claims the insurance organization is funding? GIS is a tool that provides the insurer with an accurate way to calculate acreage. Knowing exact acreage allows the insurer to save funds.

By using the suite of compatible spatial tools available from ESRI, the result is improved efficiency within the claim/payment procedure, higher customer satisfaction through an expedited response to the farmer, and the building of a spatial database related to insurance claims past and present.

Agricultural Risk Assessment with GIS

Every season that a farmer plants a crop in the field, or raises animals for meat production, there is an inherent risk to their substantial economic investment. To guard against losses, policies from insurance companies willing to underwrite these risks for a premium are an option that can be bought. How this premium is calculated by the insurance company relies heavily on tables calculated by professional actuaries. Many of the potential reasons for filing a claim against an insurance policy are geographical in nature, for example, climatic events such as hail, frost, and drought. For this reason, spatial analysis has proven useful in the calculation of the risk assessment tables and hence the fixing of insurance costs.

It would, however, be incorrect to suggest that all risk to farming investments stem from physical parameters. Other elements need to be assessed including the claim history on a specific parcel of land or field, and the current management of the farm to assess whether best practices are being used, thereby reducing risks. Although not traditionally seen as geographic in nature, these factors do have a location aspect and can be incorporated into the final assessment. Finally, more ubiquitous elements, those not really controlled substantially by location, for example, federal interest rates and global commodity prices, are incorporated. The Geostatistical Analyst extension for ArcGIS and ArcView allows scientific analysis of these factors and an ultimate calculation of risk that can vary across an agricultural landscape. Incorporating historical climatic data, claim type, and degree data allow a more accurate picture to be illustrated, with the result being a fairer assessment for farming clients.

GIS-Based Distribution Network Management for Agricultural Businesses

Crop input manufacturers use market demand models based on existing sales information and factors of influence to routinely predict future production requirements. Such companies provide primary inputs, such as fertilizer, seed, pesticides, and equipment, but can also offer services, for example, agronomic consulting, human resources for specific seasons (i.e., harvest times), and others.

An underlying principle of successful business is acquiring knowledge related to the whereabouts of assets and demands, analyzing this information, and using it to provide an optimized strategy to deliver where existing and future business opportunities are located. The term "supply chain" describes the final outcome of the above outlined steps. If a business were to implement a GIS, benefits would include maximizing replenishment efficiencies. What this means is that by calculating current and future demand for a product that requires delivery to a specific location, losses incurred by material being stored for too long at the wrong location could be minimized. A more efficient distribution network would also affect the life cycle of products, reducing them, and thus releasing asset investments and returning profits faster, improving resource accountability, and introducing an enhanced ability to match assets to specific delivery requirements on a time and location basis.

Depending on the size of the agricultural business involved, a scaled enterprise GIS solution can deliver an improved distribution network. ArcGIS, ArcSDE, ArcIMS, and ArcLogistics are fully compatible and can be connected via global positioning system (GPS), wireless telecommunication, and the Internet.

Post Harvest Processors and GIS

Companies and institutions in the industry that process raw food materials into more recognizable food products often manage huge volumes of commodities and assets across large distances and through many locations. Additionally, as agriculture becomes more regulated and responsive to public demands for greater awareness of food processing standards, improved communication within the company will not simply be advantageous but essential. Rapid data management and exchange between locations requires many integrated software solutions built around a robust data server, and the following stories describe how such systems can be implemented.

Raw Material Procurement and Delivery for the Food Processing Industry

The food processing industry relies on an accurate supply of spatial information related to markets, transportation, distribution networks, status of processing facilities, and raw material supplies to manage widely dispersed assets and maintain maximum profitability. Shortfalls or breakdowns in any part of the production chain such as redundancy at a processing facility can result in substantial losses, so ensuring timely product deliveries is essential.

Understanding the processes and movements along the transportation network from the point of production in the field to the processing facility is where GIS can assist greatly. Large food processing companies manage their operations in fine detail, contracting farmers prior to planting for delivery of specific quantities on specific dates. This management aims to reduce, as much as possible, a situation where either the processing capabilities of an asset (e.g., a mill) are underutilized or market demand outstrips production capacity. The management chain could be extended to include the delivery of the processed goods to either a retail distributor or even as far as the consumer shelf in a shop, but whether extended or not, the underlying principles remain the same.

Business models that are built and inherently contain natural phenomenon without consideration of variations outside of the control of normal land management practices are significantly weakened. The food industry is no exception and frequently suffers as a result of natural variations in such agricultural parameters as precipitation and temperature. Understanding the potential risks to agricultural production and food processing capacity relies on statistical analysis of historical information in a spatial or location-specific context. 1-Geostatistical Analyst offered as an extension of ArcGIS software provides the tools to calculate these risks and, therefore, better prepare for them when they occur.

Locating transportation assets in real time is an essential element that only becomes intensified as the perishability of the food products increases. Time constraints between harvesting a crop and delivery only increase the value and therefore the margin of profit. Managing the movement of such commodities cannot afford delays. Planning and coordinating an efficient transport network is possible by using

ArcLogistics software. GPS receivers and transmitters located on vehicles allow transport managers to better coordinate supplies to processing facilities and, consequently, enhance profitability.

Identity Preserve of Agricultural Crops

Identity Preserve is one of the fastest growing segments in agriculture and is being driven by new discoveries in biotechnology. Genetic engineering is creating crops with favorable new traits by artificially modifying plant genes. These genetically modified organisms (GMOs) impact the entire food industry. Food processors and consumers need to know whether GMO food products are being processed or consumed. In answer to these concerns Identity Preserve (IP) describes the action of tracking the agricultural products from the farm field to the grocery store shelf and indicates what these food products contain in relation to GMOs. Geoaccounting applications of Identity Preserve have demonstrated a significant benefit to agribusiness. Geoaccounting is a method to record crop input operations spatially and warehouse in a database for future reference.

The mechanics of engineering a GIS solution from the farm field to the grocery store shelf is complex, but the ArcGIS geodata model is ideally designed to be used in the creation of an intelligent polygonal object that can geoaccount transactions in the food supply chain for Identity Preserve applications.

At the high level, such as an agricultural ministry, a sophisticated application can be implemented by making all farm field parcels spatial objects within the ArcGIS/ArcSDE geodata model. This type of GIS implementation is able to maintain every transaction on each parcel, warehousing metadata, and other critical data needs required for future certification of GMO compliance regulations. An example would be a 40-hectare tract of corn. Assume it is a new corn variety, that has been genetically modified. The farm operator has chosen a GMO corn variety because his/her yields will increase by 25 percent, and the corn will be used to feed pigs. This crop input field data is archived in the GIS spatially using a polygon that begins the geoaccounting traceability functionality.

Once the metadata and learned object behavior (geoaccounting) is in place at the farm parcel level, the geoaccounting of the GMOs shifts to the nonspatial, supply chain business process models. These supply chain models need to be spatially enabled. The crop is removed from the farm field, and the product becomes a point feature within the supply chain. This point is still a spatial representation of the GMO or non-GMO commodity in the food supply chain. The collection of this information can be done at the field level by using ArcPad. The crop now leaves the farm field and begins its transport through the supply chain by truck to the local grain elevator for storage, then by barge, then by shipping container, then by multiple shipping vessels to processing plants and then distributed as value-added food products (e.g., wheat grain processed into flour) to the grocery store shelf. Tracking this movement can be assisted greatly by the implementation of an ArcIMS/ ArcGIS solution. Segregating the GMO from the non-GMO products will, over time, be certified on the food label, and will satisfy growing consumer concerns regarding the health implication of GMO products. By using GIS, the crop's identity can be tracked or traced throughout the supply chain by GPS, bar code, passive infrared sensor, or other inexpensive technologies. The crop, whether GMO or not, always has a location value—from the farm, through the transportation of the commodity, to the grocery store shelf. Using the powerful network features of ArcGIS lets the agribusiness or agricultural government agency manage the identity of the commodities thorough the food supply chain.

By knowing the location of the crop throughout the food supply chain, manufacturers can benefit from being able to assure consumers as to the legacy of any particular product either via food labeling or more interactive technologies in-store.

Access to Secondary Data via a Geography Network

The Internet has removed many of the barriers to communication associated with distance. Providing data to a larger audience, whether public or corporate, is just one of the consequences. Agribusiness can benefit from this data dissemination by either creating internal distribution networks or accessing data services provided by third party groups. The Geography Network architecture allows these data transactions to be executed. Spatial data can be made freely available to all users of a company's Intranet for incorporation in decision making processes. Connecting to the Internet allows new data to be acquired from other data providers as well as providing a portal through which potential data customers can view data on a host machine.

The software used to operate Geography Network includes ArcIMS and ArcSDE software. ArcIMS is used to create, publish, and administer the map services. ArcSDE is used to store and deliver the geographic data used to support the map services. A typical system hardware configuration includes a server-class machine that houses the Web, mapping, and data servers.

To facilitate both internal and external geography networks, tools have been placed in ArcGIS enabling users to access and use geographic information on the Geography Network. Users will be able to access data directly through their desktop applications or Web browsers and integrate it with local data. The ability to incorporate multiple data sets in ArcGIS and access it by way of the Geography Network will facilitate more participation and collaboration in the decision making that affects agricultural industries around the world.

Agricultural Research and GIS

Necessity might well be the mother of invention, and agricultural science is no exception. Even though research into agriculture has been carried out for millenia, increasing demand for agricultural products caused by population growth and a growing environmental awareness means that research must be continued. Spatial analysis facilitated by implementing GIS tools offers researchers new and exciting approaches to answer some of mankind's oldest questions.

Spatializing Agronomic Modeling

Agricultural production is wholly related to a crop's interaction with the environment in which it is situated. Such an obvious statement seems redundant until it is understood that the majority of current agronomic models do not contain a spatial component. Attempting to understand and quantify the effect that variations in climate, substrate, water availability, and management have on a harvest has occupied scientific research for many years. The successful result of any agronomic model is the ability to predict how a specific crop will behave under varying conditions and then extrapolate this information throughout a broader landscape. The spatialization of agronomic models can be achieved by combining physiological information related to the crop, environmental conditions, and management practices within a geographic information system.

Collecting enough information at a suitable scale for the implementation of a spatialized agronomic model is challenging. Decisions need to be made defining the scales at which results from the model can be extrapolated. Indicating a scale too large can cause excessive detail in the final analysis, rendering the model ineffective, while including information of a smaller scale can cause problems associated with data generalization.

GIS provides not only a means to incorporate data layers from many scientific disciplines and display them but a method to include within traditional agronomic studies a spatial component at the heart of any agronomic model. The Geostatistical Analyst extension for ArcGIS provides the tools by which a researcher can quantify the degree to which a specific parameter affects the overall production of a crop. The ModelBuilder extension allows scientists to interactively create new agronomic models using a simple interface that can include both vectorized and rasterized data sets. Spatial regression analysis is key to extrapolating results from existing or future agronomic models and will continue to grow in importance as the relationship between crop productivity and location is reexamined.

Land Suitability Evaluation Supported by GIS

Agricultural suitability mapping involves identifying land use patterns and assessing whether the current use is the most feasible both economically and environmentally. Essential to such activities is an accurate inventory of current land use. Asset mapping, like all other agricultural practices, is scale dependent, so various strategies for different study scales should be employed. A factor, however, that does not change with scale, whether it is at the subfield or national level, is that improved knowledge of what exists allows for better management practices.

Useful suitability assessments cannot solely be based upon biophysical resource information. Other factors include transportation networks, scale dependent localized economies, and social factors such as education and demographics. Obviously, large volumes of spatially related information need to be efficiently managed. The GIS required to service such research must incorporate high functionality and an ability to work seamlessly with both raster and vector data structures. Tabular information from census and agricultural statistics, raster image data, and vectorized productivity field data all add elements to the overall study. Such data integration, however, is only half of the story, and equal efforts need be applied in mapping and understanding relationships evident in the compiled information. Crop modeling, including soil/water requirement and geostatistical analysis, is critical at this stage to identify and make sense of complicated spatial relationships and, ultimately, substantiate trends and theories.

Looking at this abbreviated description of the processes involved in agricultural suitability mapping, it would be easy to become distracted from the ultimate aim, that of providing decision makers, whether farmers or politicians, with improved tools to aid land management and policy making processes.

Building Agricultural Land Management Scenarios with GIS

Land management practices in agricultural areas need to be seriously considered and researched before they are ever implemented. Maintaining the status quo can, in some situations, be as damaging to the farmland as ill-thought, out-of-state policy decisions. Either at the local farm level or at national scales, events outside of the control of the farmer can have substantial impact on a person's livelihood. Climatic change, increased population pressure, and legislation controlling certain farming activities and commodity prices are but a sample of events that need to be considered. So how does an agricultural researcher evaluate and measure the impact of these influences and subsequently develop new and successful farm management scenarios? One solution comes in the form of computer modeling and implementing a GIS to take into consideration the natural variations found in any piece of farmland.

If we consider the reasons that applied research is performed, for example the development of a successful land management decision support system, any results would primarily serve the user, whether a farmer or policy maker, to assess potential risks and opportunities.

What benefits are apparent that would create the need for research to be carried out at the farm level? By mapping a farm's attributes at the field level and including knowledge regarding input costs, potential returns for different crops, and probabilities of climatic conditions, the researcher can build potential impact scenarios. By analyzing these results, options can be provided to the farmer, based on a predetermined acceptable level of risk. Agricultural crop modeling can be included to demonstrate potential effects from events such as a flood or frost.

On a smaller scale a watershed or county district indications of the relative importance of the variability of both biophysical and cultural landscape attributes could be included.

From predicting the livestock carrying capacity of extensive rangelands to providing managers with soil erosion risk indicators, the spatial analysis capabilities found within a GIS can greatly assist research staff in answering the questions demanded of them.

Agrobiodiversity and GIS

Since man first domesticated wild varieties of wheat and barley, breeding techniques have focused on the selection of desirable physical traits to improve crop quality and productivity. These methods are as relevant today as they were 5,000 years ago, but are being supplemented by the new technology represented by GMOs. To supply farmers and researchers alike with the genetic material to improve crop species under current and future conditions, scientists have collected germ plasm and acted as guardians for centuries. In situ conservation marks a new approach whereby useful germ plasm is maintained in its native environment as opposed to more traditional seed banks. GIS offers exciting possibilities that include the documentation of sites and locations of potential collection areas based on varying biophysical parameters and assessing risk to genetically diverse locations.

GIS software is employed in many conservation projects around the world. The power that GIS brings to the efficient documentation of such activities is often sufficient justification when the number of seemingly disparate data layers is considered. Moreover, spatial analysis greatly helps in the planning phase of such projects a methodology that ultimately leads to a successful implementation.

Utilizing GIS in a coordinated manner has proven to be the ultimate management tool for the exploration, exploitation, and conservation of genetic material essential to the development of improved varieties of basic food commodities.

Implementing GIS in Government

National institutions that oversee agriculture at the governmental level have a multifaceted responsibility to a wide range of seemingly disparate groups. All the way through the food supply chain from farmer to consumer, agricultural ministries and departments collect, collate, manage, and disseminate information. Such activities are only going to increase with growing public awareness of farming practices and resultant legislation.

If there is a foreseen overriding theme in new efforts to better manage agriculture, it might be communication, not just between government and consumer but also internally. While not being the whole solution, GIS can assist, and the following is a selection of applications where GIS has been implemented to move toward this goal.

Agricultural Subsidy Procedures Facilitated by GIS

Agriculturalists in many developed countries rely heavily on subsidy payments to assist in maintaining viable commercial operations. In 1998, the European Union paid the equivalent of $39 billion (U.S.) to its farmers as part of the Common Agricultural Policy (CAP). Annual operational costs for such schemes are huge, and methods to improve efficiency by even 1 percent can have profound economic benefits.

Subsidy claims have four distinct phases. The farmer first needs to be provided with the necessary information if the application is to be processed smoothly. By definition, rural areas tend to be less accessible, so information exchange can be hindered. The farmer then fills out the forms and submits them to the relevant governmental office, either the Ministry of Agriculture or the State Agricultural Commissioner's office. The claim is processed and verification is then carried out, sometimes using satellite imagery, but more often than not by field inspectors. Once the verification has been completed, payments are released to the claimants. The required communication to see this process through is great, and delays can result from misplaced or misdirected information.

The use of the Internet in rural areas has witnessed rapid growth as areas previously considered less accessible come online. To the farming community, this will become even more important. Governments now have the option to reach an increasing group of agricultural subsidy claimants via the Web. Internet sites offering advice on governmental procedures are not uncommon, and with time the departments associated with agriculture will increase their visibility. The application for subsidies can now be theoretically done online, thus saving costs for printed materials and postage. Fields are often the land unit most associated with claims, and by using ArcIMS technologies, farmers will be able to locate their field on a map service and fill in the details directly to a server. The volume of information stored on the spatial servers will necessitate a high server/client performance. ArcSDE (Spatial Database Engine) software is capable of delivering this performance. The mechanism of data transfer means that data entered by the farmer via the online claim form is automatically written to the database. This eliminates the need for data entry at the processing institution, thereby reducing costs and potential errors in data input. As many subsidy payments depend on historical land information on a parcel-by-parcel basis, this information could also be included so that rules governing the validity of claims could be built-in at the data entry level. This would indicate to the farmer when it was known that the claim in its current form would be inadmissible, thereby reducing the need to send the information back to the farmer for correction and allowing immediate correction. Although satellite imagery is used more frequently in the verification process, portable GIS technology is invaluable for field scouts. ArcPad, the mobile GIS software, can be customized to create specific forms for data input; information can then be uploaded from the field wirelessly to the central server over the Internet if necessary.

Information exchange is always a challenge throughout such a complex procedure. Using ArcIMS means that once claims have been submitted, farmers could check online using digital maps of their farmland to see what stage the process has reached. Such an enterprise GIS solution requires research, investment, and maintenance, but potential financial benefits and process efficiency would prove significant.

Centralizing Agricultural Data Management for Policy Development

Perhaps the biggest questions that arise when both individuals and institutions contact government agricultural agencies for specific information, whether spatial or otherwise, are where is the data, and with whom do I communicate to get it? The answers to these apparently straightforward questions are often well hidden within agency bureaucracy and institutional structure. A data management system, full of incompatible software frequently developed in-house, does not produce industry-standard data formats and was never designed initially to hold data in a spatial context.

The answer is facilitated by a compatible set of industry-standard software tools that work individually but, when combined, provide a complete and professional solution. The ESRI product family, including ArcGIS 8.x, ArcIMS, and ArcSDE, delivers just such a scalable solution and brings with it a pedigree of software developed for governmental applications.

It must be accepted that the majority of agricultural commissioners, ministries, and departments are both made up of regional offices and generate large volumes of agricultural data. Using the ESRI enterprise solution, these offices are able to fulfill their existing responsibilities while updating a centralized data catalog via an Intranet or even the Internet. Decision support for both routine and emergency operations benefits from the seamless transfer of data that the solution provides. Internet access of the cataloged data holdings means that both farmers and agricultural government employees can more fully assist in both regional and local agricultural management strategies.

Internet GIS Assists Crop Input Permitting

Restrictions controlling the application of certain chemical inputs, such as fertilizers or pesticides, imposed on farmers will increase as environmental concerns figure more heavily in agricultural management. Increased legislation inevitably leads to more cost for both farmer and regulatory bodies. By taking advantage of a permitting process available across the Internet, the farmer can reduce the time needed to make field-based permit applications and free up time for other tasks.

The Agricultural Commissioner can streamline and reduce departmental transaction costs associated with permitting by utilizing a GIS and the Internet. Using ESRI's ArcIMS, farmers seeking permission to apply chemicals to individual fields can do so by using a custom-built, interactive mapping tool that is located on the Commissioner's Internet home page. Once an application for a permit has been received and reviewed, the Commissioner can utilize the same Internet Web page to inform the farmer of the outcome of his or her application graphically on a field-by-field basis.

The amount of information that needs to be handled at a county or state level would justify the use of ArcSDE. Benefits would be twofold: the volume of spatial data transactions generated could be easily accommodated while the update of the spatial database would occur simultaneously with the digital application of the farmer, eliminating any chance of data entry duplication.

Government and the Agricultural Land Parcel

A simple agricultural field in the countryside often represents a great number of paper transactions that are generally carried out at state and local government levels. Activities associated with land parcel zoning dictate its use within a community; however, these rules are not set in stone, and with time, these land use priorities can change. Such reallocation of land use classification, or variance as it is known, is often a protracted procedure involving many agencies and individuals. Communication is the lubrication necessary between all parties to advance constructively toward an accepted concensus. Governments around the world are discovering the benefits that the Internet can bring to any procedure involving public comment and feedback, and agricultural government is no exception. The rural setting of the majority of agricultural communities has traditionally been less accessible, but the Internet is able to bridge such physical constraints. By combining GIS and the Internet, governmental agricultural offices can inform the public of many different activities that previously relied on personal visits or printed materials. A front-end Web page created using ArcIMS linked to a server running ArcSDE allows the public to access all the relevant information for the parcel of land in which they have an interest. All the relevant data can be stored on a server, providing answers more cost effectively to citizens' questions regarding land taxation, agricultural water rights, and land ownership.

In many parts of the world, agricultural water rights play an important role in development. Once ownership has been established, such applications as the issuance of drilling permits for irrigation purposes or the enforcement of effluent management, legislation leading to liability being established for individuals or groups that do not comply can be carried out.

GIS Bites into Agricultural Government

Compliance Programs for Crop Inputs: Although crop inputs take many forms, pesticides pose the greatest hazard to the environment and, for this reason, state agricultural agencies must carefully manage pesticide applications to achieve an acceptable balance between the economic interests of the farming community and the health of the larger community. Regulation of pesticide use varies from state to state, but all states require the collection of information such as how much and where pesticides have been applied. Because much of this information is tied to a discrete land parcel or field, it can be most easily stored and manipulated spatially. Storing this information within a GIS allows state officials to better manage the permit application process, perform water quality monitoring, and investigate point source pollution events.

Pest Control: Integrated pest management relies on accurate data related to the quantity and location of pests within a county. Using insect traps and field observations, government entomologists identify infestations and recommend remedial measures. GIS plays an important role in data collection, interpolation, and analysis. Data can be gathered in the field on handheld units running ArcPad, analyzed in the office using ArcView, and disseminated using ArcIMS to send farmers current information on pest outbreak locations, areas of potential risk, and recommendations for eradication. A public Web page supplies real-time information that can reduce the impact of infestations.

Business Licensing for Food Processors: Large food processing and production facilities must comply with governmental guidelines for hygiene, operating conditions, and product quality. From initial license application to issuance, GIS helps agencies communicate and work with food companies. GIS can provide inspectors with optimized route and map information for premises to be inspected and allow real-time central database updates of data collected from handheld devices running GIS. These benefits result in better planning and service to both the food industry and the consumer.

GIS for Archaeology

Research

GIS is a powerful tool for density analysis of selected features or artifact types across a site, or of site types across a region. Use ArcGIS Spatial Analyst to analyze clustering, proximity, orientation, intervisibility, and other spatial relationships.

Visualize these patterns and relationships with ArcGlobe, part of the ArcGIS 3D Analyst extension. ArcGlobe provides continuous, multi resolution, interactive viewing of geographic information. Like ArcMap, ArcGlobe works with GIS data layers, displaying information from a geodatabase and all supported GIS data formats.

Survey and Excavation

By using Mobile ArcGIS Desktop Systems running on a laptop or tablet PC, you can increase your mapping and data recording speed at the excavation site and gain immediate access to the day's data for analysis and visualization.

Building a site GIS allows you to interact with your excavation data visually and to merge data from multiple sources, such as surface survey, geophysical and remote sensing equipment, and excavation. Archaeologists are increasingly turning to GIS for field data recording, either using handheld computers and ArcPad, or ArcView running on a tablet PC or laptop.

Data Management

ArcCatalog, an ArcGIS Desktop Application, gives you the tools to explore and manage your data holdings.

Mulitple users can have read and write access to the same database with ArcSDE, a server software product that provides a suite of services that enhance data management performance. Visualize your data using ArcMap and ArcGlobe in a resource management or permitting content, or for a project, and publish dynamic maps onine using ArcIMS.

Modeling

3 D Modeling

GIS gives you the tools to excavate a site, digitize/record each stratum or level as it is removed, and rebuild a 3D virtual site. From the 3D model, you can view layers individually or in combination to compare data and identify spatial relationships. Using ArcGIS 3D Analyst, you can review site area and structure volume statistics.

Predictive Modeling

GIS has most frequently been employed in archaeological studies for large-scale regional analyses and predictive modeling of settlement patterns and land use. ArcGIS Spatial Analyst gives you the capabilities to search for and uncover patterns.

Public Education/Museums

Museums and heritage management organizations are using the Internet and Internet map servers to open up archaeological and historic preservation GIS data on the Web.

ArcIMS delivers dynamic maps over the Web, making it easy to share maps and data with a wide audience. Maps can be viewed in a standard Web browser without special software or plug-ins. ArcIMS samples and Site Starter applications make it easy to build a new site quickly and begin publishing your maps in minutes.

ArcGIS Publisher and ArcReader make it easy to share publication-quality maps freely while maintaining the interactivity of GIS. ArcReader is a free application that provides map navigation, search, and hyperlink functions for maps created with ArcGIS and published through ArcGIS Publisher.

ArcWeb Services provide access to geographic data and GIS capabilities through the Web environment, giving you on-demand access to GIS.

GIS for Telecommunications

GIS can enhance the decision process by combining appropriate groups of business and consumers, existing infrastructure, and right-of-ways.

GIS technology enables telecommunication professionals to integrate location-based data into analysis and management processes in network planning and operations, marketing and sales, customer care, data management, and many other planning and problem-solving tasks. A GIS can integrate location-based data from databases all over the world to help you resolve and streamline everyday business tasks.

Streamlining the Enterprise

Using GIS to Manage Corporate Data

Better Decision Making: Telecommunication and location service companies network deployments by combining market segmentation, network planning and engineering databases. The decision where to rollout networks first has an enormous impact on the organization. Geographic locations, as well as the package of services, are the two most crucial decision points in a telecommunication or location service business. The combination of the appropriate groups of business and consumers, existing infrastructure, and right-of-ways creates a location-based decision process, a process that GIS can enhance and simplify.

Faster Network Rollout: Once strategic network deployment decisions are made, enterprise GIS streamlines the organization. GIS greatly reduces the number of meetings between departments during the process because the status of network rollout is constantly available to all parties concerned.

Competitive Advantage: Better decisions and faster rollout enable the organization to capitalize on new telecommunication and location service technologies. The fastest and easiest way to gain market share is to offer a service before competitors do. Enterprise GIS enables you to do just that.

Customer Relationship Management

Customer Relationship Management (CRM) is the crucial interface between a telecommunications carrier and its customers and prospects. GIS gives call center operators an instant view of a customer location, nearby facilities, requests for services, and signal quality. GIS dramatically reduces service request turnaround times by integrating historical network and customer data with a Trouble Ticketing system.

Marketing and Sales

GIS allows marketers to use vital consumer and business statistics geographically, to provide input to capacity planning applications, and to direct targeted marketing campaigns. Telecommunications sales representatives can get quick customer profiles using geographic questions such as:

- Where is the customer?
- Which products and services are in use?
- What is the distance to the nearest fiber backbone?
- When do we plan to have coverage at this location?

Network Planning

Network capacity planning with GIS takes a high-level view of network performance and trends to effectively plan new or additional facilities. In this process, companies define priorities by mapping out existing infrastructure, zoning, customer data, and topography.

Wireless Engineering

ESRI GIS provides highly efficient support of wireless engineering and fixed wireless engineering programs. The leading radio frequency (RF) engineering software manufacturers have adopted the ESRI GIS platform to manage and distribute their geographic data for their applications. ESRI software integrates RF engineering applications into your enterprise work flow.

Operations Support Systems

Operations Support Systems (OSS) use GIS to monitor and evaluate network performance, to dispatch service vehicles, and to follow network testing. ArcInfo and ArcIMS enable network replication, near real-time monitoring, tracking, and storage of network-related data. You can disseminate that information using ArcIMS on the corporate Intranet.

GIS for Water and Wastewater Management

GIS gives you an intelligent database that integrates job planning, equipment inventory, and flow analysis into one system.

GIS is a powerful tool in helping you manage the flow of water and wastewater to service homes and businesses. You can also use GIS technology to track the location and condition of water mains, valves, hydrants, meters, storage facilities, sewer mains, and manholes. This same technology makes keeping up with NPDES compliance, TV inspection data, and condition ratings easier.

A majority of water/wastewater utilities use GIS technology to integrate all kinds of information and applications with a geographic component into one, manageable system. GIS allows you to organize, manage, and distribute geographic information culled from various databases while maintaining data integrity and focusing on project direction.

GIS for Infrastructure Management and Construction

Water and wastewater organizations are often responsible for constructing and/or overseeing the development of new facilities and replacement of old facilities. GIS aids in tracking information related to projects, permits, construction work order management, inspections, as-built, and so forth.

Dynamic segmentation and image integration features in GIS allow utilities to store and display images in conjunction with a footage reading and a description of the pipe defect (roots, grease, other problems). Maps, drawings, and pictures can also be associated with valves, manholes, drop inlets, and other features to provide valuable information to the user.

GIS for Finance and Administration

Finance and Administration provides the central administrative oversight to support the planning and operational activities of the organization. Budget forecasting, facility inventory analysis, customer billing, and other key administrative functions can be enhanced through the implementation of an integrated, enterprise wide GIS solution.

GIS can be used for tasks such as

- Rate justification
- Capital improvement project tracking
- Customer information service
- Complaint tracking
- Real property
- Redistricting

GIS for Operations and Maintenance

Many utilities have discovered the value of GIS for improving day-to-day operations. GIS can be used to closely model utility networks and integrate other related types of data such as raster images and CAD drawings. GIS spatial selection and display tools allow users to visualize scheduled work, ongoing activities, recurring maintenance problems, and historical information.

The topological characteristics of a GIS database can support network tracing and can be used to analyze specific properties or services that may be impacted by such events as stoppages, main breaks, drainage defects, and so forth. Dynamic segmentation can also be used to derive a generalized network that combines hydraulically similar sections into larger strips to make pressure and flow analysis algorithms run more efficiently. GIS can perform many other operations and maintenance tasks, including work order and warehouse inventory management and SCADA.

GIS for Planning and Engineering

Water agencies use GIS from ESRI to map the full extent of their water distribution systems and link them to a database defining each element including reservoirs, pipe segments, services, and system appurtenances.

GIS provides you with an intelligent database so that job planning, equipment inventory, and flow analysis become an automated procedure integrated into one system. You can link your current network modeling system to the GIS, tie it to the attribute data, and map the results.

ESRI's GIS software allows you to represent a project in three-dimensional form to visualize the impact of facilities on landscape during the design process. This data can then be combined with other computer-aided engineering functions to assist the engineering designer in the planning and scenario testing of various designs.

Planning and engineering tasks that can be accomplished easily using ESRI's GIS software include

- Watershed modeling
- Water distribution system master planning
- Population and demand projections
- Groundwater management/modeling
- Water quality monitoring
- Hazardous materials tracking/underground tank management
- Well log and data management
- Site analysis
- Geobibliography (past studies)
- Development review and approval
- Right-of-way engineering
- Water flow analysis
- Automated mapping
- Capital improvement project tracking
- Underground service alert

Bibliography

Achard, F. and F. Blasco. 1990. Analysis of vegetation seasonal evolution and mapping of forest cover in West Africa with the use of NOAA AVHRR HRPT data. *Photogrammetric Engineering and Remote Sensing* 56: 1359–65.

Anderson, W., W. Wentz, and B. Treadwell. 1985. Una guía sobre informacióndе sensores remotos para biólogos especializados en vida silvestre. In R. Rubén, ed., *Manual de Técnicas de GestióndeVida Silvestre*, 305–20. Bethesda, Md.: The Wildlife Society.

Bauer, M. E., T. E. Burk, A. R. Ek, P. R. Coppin, S. D. Lime, T. A. Walsh, D. K. Walters, W. Befort, and D. F. Heinzen. 1994. Satellite inventory of Minnesota forest resources. *Photogrammetric Engineering and Remote Sensing* 60: 287–98.

Bolaños, R. A. and V. C. Watson. 1993. *Mapa de Zonas de Vida de Costa Rica: Hojas Liberia y Nicoya. Escala 1:200.000* (Ecological map of life zones in Costa Rica: [According to the

Calvopiña, J. 1990. Reintroducción del venado cola blanca (*Odocoileus virginianus)* a Cobano, Puntareanas, Costa Rica. Tesis de Maestría, Sistema de Estudios de Postgrado, Programa Regional en Manejo de Vida Silvestre. Heredia, C.R.: Universidad Nacional.

Chomentowski, W., B. Salas, and D. Skole. 1994. Landsat pathfinder project advances deforestation mapping. *GIS World* (April): 34–8.

Demarchi, D. 1986. *Biophysical habitat mapping: Draft methodology.* Victoria, B.C.: Mapping Standards Committee, Ministry of Environment.

Eastman, J. R. 1992. *IDRISI (Version 4.0)*. Worcester, Mass.: Clark University.

Eggen-McIntosh, S., K. B. Lannom, and Z. Zhu. 1993. Study plan: Development of forest

Ehlers, M., M. A. Jadkowski, R. R. Howard, and D. E. Brostuen. 1990. Application of SPOT data for regional growth analysis and local planning. *Photogrammetric Engineering and Remote Sensing* 56: 175–80.

Evans, D. L., Z. Zhu, S. Eggen-McIntosh, P. G. Mayoral, and J. L. O. de Anda. 1992b. *Mapping Mexico's forest lands with advanced very high resolution radiometer*. Washington, D.C.: U.S. Forest Service Research Note, SO-367.

Gallina, S. 1995. Uso del hábitat por el venado cola blanca en la Reserva de la Biosfera La Michilia, México. In C. Vaughan and M. Rodàguez, eds., *Ecologia y Manejo del Venado Cola Blanca en Mexico y Costa Rica*, 299–314. Heredia, C.R.: Editorial UNA.

Gaudette, M. and D. Stauffer. 1988. Assessing habitat of white-tailed deer in Southwestern Virginia. *Wildlife Society Bulletin* 16: 284–90.

Gilruth, P. T., C. F. Hutchinson, and B. Berry. 1990. Assessing deforestation in the Guinea highlands of West Africa using remote sensing. *Photogrammetric Engineering and Remote Sensing* 56: 1375–82.

Graham, L. 1993. Airborne video for near-real-time vegetation mapping. *Journal of Forestry* 91(8): 28–32.

Green, K. M., J. F. Lynch, J. Sircar, and L. S. Z. Greenberg. 1987. Landsat remote sensing to assess habitat for migratory birds in the Yucatan Peninsula, Mexico. *Vida Silvestre Neotropical* 1(2): 27–38.

Gysel, L. and L. Lyon. 1985. Análisis y evaluación del hábitat. In R. Rubén, ed., *Manual de Técnicas de Gestióndе Vida Silvestre*, 321–44. Bethesda, Md.: The Wildlife Society.

Halls, L. 1984. Research problems and needs. In L. Halls, ed., *White-tailed Deer: Ecology and Management*, 783–90. Harrisburg, Penn.: Stackpole.

Hastings, D. A. and W. J. Emery. 1992. The advanced very high resolution radiometer (AVHRR): A brief reference guide. *Photogrammetric Engineering and Remote Sensing* 58: 1183–88.

Hastings, D. A., M. Matson, and A. H. Horbitz. 1989. AVHRR. *Photogrammetric Engineering and Remote Sensing* 55(2): 168–69.

Irwin, L. and J. Cook. 1985. Determining appropriate variables for a habitat suitability model for pronghorns. *Wildlife Society Bulletin* 13: 434–40.

Jackson, L. L. 1992. The role of ecological restoration in conservation biology. In P. L. Fiedler and S. K. Jain, eds., *Conservation biology*, 433–51. New York: Chapman and Hall.

Janzen, D. F. H. 1988. Tropical ecological and biocultural restoration. *Science* 239: 243–44.

Jensen, J. R. 1995. *Introductory digital image processing: A remote sensing perspective.* 2d ed. Englewood Cliffs, N.J.: Prentice-Hall.

Johnson, K. 1994. Segment-based land-use classification from SPOT satellite data. *Photogrammetric Engineering and Remote Sensing* 60: 47–53.

Jones, J. R. 1992. Environmental issues and policies in Costa Rica: Control of deforestation. *Policy Studies Journal* 20: 679–94.

Joria, P. E., S. C. Ahearn, and M. Connor. 1991. A comparison of the SPOT and Landsat Thematic Mapper satellite systems for detecting gypsy moth defoliation in Michigan. *Photogrammetric Engineering and Remote Sensing* 57: 1605–12.

Kidwell, K. B. 1988. *NOAA polar orbiter data (TIROS-N, NOAA-7, NOAA-8, NOAA-9, NOAA-10, and NOAA-11) users guide.* Washington, D.C.: National Oceanic and Atmospheric Administration.

Leonard, H. J. 1987. *Natural resources and economic development in Central America: A regional environmental profile.* New Brunswick, N.J.: Transaction Books.

Lillesand, T. M. and R. W. Kiefer. 1994. *Remote sensing and image interpretation.* New York: Wiley.

Loveland, T. R., J. W. Merchant, D. O. Ohlen, and J. F. Brown. 1991. Development of a land-cover characteristics database for the conterminous U.S. *Photogrammetric Engineering and Remote Sensing* 57: 1453–63.

Matulich, S., J. Hanson, I. Lines, and A. Farmer. 1982. HEP as a planning tool: An application to waterfowl enhancement. *Transactions of the North American Wildlife and Natural Resources Conference* 47: 111–27.

Moran, E. F., E. Brondizio, P. Mausel, and Y. Wu. 1994. Integrating Amazonian vegetation, land-use, and satellite data. *BioScience* 44: 329–38.

Mulders, M. A., S. De Bruin, and B. P. Schuiling. 1992. Structured approach to land cover mapping of the Atlantic zone of Costa Rica using single date TM data. *International Journal of Remote Sensing* 13: 3017–33.

O'Neill, T. 1993. New sensors eye the rain forest. *National Geographic* (September): 118–24.

Parker, W. 1990. A proposal to reintroduce the red wolf to the Great Smoky Mountains National Park. In *Proceedings, First Annual Southern Appalachian Man and the Biosphere Conference*, 53. Norris, Tenn.: Tennessee Valley Authority.

Patton, D. 1984. A model to evaluate Abert squirrel habitat in uneven-aged ponderosa pine. *Wildlife Society Bulletin* 12: 408–14.

Pohl, C. 1995. Updating Indonesian maps using SPOT/ERS image maps. *SPOT Magazine* 24: 17–19.

Pope, K. O., J. M. Rey-Benayas, and J. F. Paris. 1994. Radar remote sensing of forest and wetland ecosystems in the Central American tropics. *Remote Sensing of Environment* 48: 205–19.

Powell, G. V. N., J. H. Rappole, and S. A. Sader. 1989. Neotropical migrant landbird use of lowland Atlantic habitats in Costa Rica: A test of remote sensing for identification of habitat. In *Manomet Symposium*, 287–98. Washington, D.C.: Smithsonian Institution Press.

Prasad, S. N., R. S. Chundawat, D. O. Hunter, H. S. Panwar, and G. S. Rawat. 1991. Remote sensing snow leopard habitat in the trans-Himalaya of India using spatial models and satellite imagery—preliminary results. *Proceedings, Resource Technology '90, 2nd International Symposium on Advanced Technology in Natural Resources Management*, 519– 23. Bethesda, Md.: American Society for Photogrammetry and Remote Sensing.

Rasch, H. 1994. Mapping of vegetation, land cover, and land use by satellite—experience and conclusions for future project applications. *Photogrammetric Engineering and Remote Sensing* 60: 265–71.

Rhodes, M., T. Cloud, and D. Haag. 1983. Habitat evaluation procedures for planning surface mine reclamation in Texas. *Wildlife Society Bulletin* 11: 222–32.

Ringrose, S. M. and P. Large. 1983. The comparative value of Landsat print and digitized data and radar imagery for ecological land classification in the humid tropics. *Canadian Journal of Remote Sensing* 9: 435–60.

Rodàguez, M., C. Vaughan, V. Villalobos, and M. McCoy. 1985. Notas sobre los movimientos del venado cola blanca. In G. Estrella, ed., *Investigaciones sobre Fauna Silvestre de Costa Rica*, 37–46. San José, C.R.: Editorial Universidad Estatal a Distancia.

Roller, N. E. G. and J. E. Colwell. 1986. Coarse-resolution satellite data for ecological surveys. *BioScience* 36: 468–75.

Sader, S. A. and A. T. Joyce. 1988. Deforestation rates and trends in Costa Rica, 1940 to 1983. *Biotropica* 20: 11–19.

Sader, S. A., T. A. Stone, and A. T. Joyce. 1990. Remote sensing of tropical forests: An overview of research and applications using non-photographic sensors. *Photogrammetric Engineering and Remote Sensing* 56: 1343–51.

Saénz, J. 1990. Ecologíade dos grupos de venados cola blanca (*Odocoileus virginianus*) liberados en un nuevo hábitat. Tesis de grado: Ingenieríaen Ciencias Forestales, Grado Académico Licenciado, EDECA. Heredia, C.R.: Universidad Nacional.

Schamberger, M. and A. Farmer. 1978. The habitat evaluation procedures: Their application in project planning and impact evaluation. *Transactions of the North American Wildlife and Natural Resources Conference* 43: 275–83.

Scott, J. M., F. Davis, B. Csuti, B. Butterfield, R. Noss, S. Caicco, H. Anderson, J. Ulliman, F. D'Erchia, and C. Groves. 1990. *Gap analysis: Protecting biodiversity using geographic information systems.* A handbook prepared for a workshop held at the University of Idaho, Moscow.

Scott, J. M., F. Davis, B. Csuti, R. Noss, B. Butterfield, C. Groves, H. Anderson, S. Caicco, F. D'Erchia, T. C. Edwards Jr., J. Ulliman, and R. G. Wright. 1993. *Gap analysis: A geographical approach to protection of biological diversity.* Wildlife Monograph no. 123 (41 pp.). Bethesda, Md.: The Wildlife Society.

Thomas, J. 1982. Needs for and approaches to wildlife habitat assessment. *Transactions of the North American Wildlife and Natural Resources Conference* 47: 35–46.

Townshend, J. R. G. and C. O. Justice. 1986. Analysis of the dynamics of African vegetation using the normalized difference vegetation index. *International Journal of Remote Sensing* 7: 1435–45.

Trimble Navigation. 1992. *Operating the GPS Pathfinder basic receivers.* Sunnyvale, Calif.: Trimble Navigation.

Tucker, C. J., B. N. Holben, and T. E. Goff. 1984. Intensive forest clearing in Rondonia, Brazil, as detected by satellite remote sensing. *Remote Sensing of Environment* 15: 255–61.

U.S. Fish and Wildlife Service. 1991. *Habitat evaluation procedures (HEP).* Washington, D.C.: Division of Ecological Services, Department of the Interior.

Ward,L. and B. Weigle. 1993. To save a species: GIS for manatee research and management. *GIS World* 6: 34–37.

Welch, R., M. Remillard, and R. Slack. 1988. Remote sensing and geographic information system techniques for aquatic resource evaluation. *Photogrammetric Engineering and Remote Sensing* 54: 177–85.

Williamson, S. and D. Hirth. 1985. An evaluation of edge use by white-tailed deer. *Wildllife Society Bulletin* 13: 252–57.

INDEX